PERT TEST READING AND WRITING SUCCESS

Florida PERT Test Preparation Book

© COPYRIGHT 2008-2014. Academic Success Media DBA www.college-placement-test.com
All rights reserved. No part of this publication may be reproduced, stored in a retrieval system, or transmitted, in any form or by any means, electronic, mechanical, photocopying, recording, or otherwise.

COPYRIGHT NOTICE TO EDUCATORS: Please respect copyright law. Under no circumstances may you make copies of these materials for distribution to students. Should you wish to use the materials in a classroom, you are legally required to purchase a copy for each of your students.

Note: PERT and the Postsecondary Educational Readiness Test are trademarks of McCann Testing. Neither McCann Testing nor the Florida Department of Education are affiliated with or endorse this publication.

You may also be interested in our other publication entitled:

PERT Math Test Success

TABLE OF CONTENTS

PERT Test Format   1

PERT Reading Test Information and Tips   2

PERT Writing Test Information and Tips   4

PERT Reading Test 1:

    Selection 1 – Teenage Smoking   6

    Selection 2 – Ancient Cosmetics   7

    Selection 3 – The Function of the Actor   8

    Selection 4 – The Power of Tornadoes   9

    Selection 5 – Marie Curie and the Discovery of Radium   10

    Selection 6 – Credit Card Spending and Personal Finance   12

    Selection 7 – Mount Rushmore in the Black Hills   13

    Selection 8 – Excerpt from *The Yellow Wallpaper*   15

    Selection 9 – Computers and the Stock Market   16

    Selection 10 – The Law of Perpetual Motion   17

    Selection 11 – Excerpt from the State v. Scopes Trial   17

    Selection 12 – Radioactive Waste   18

    Selection 13 – Excerpt from *Robinson Crusoe*   19

    Selection 14 – Multiple Intelligences   20

    Selection 15 – Michelangelo and the Sistine Chapel   21

    Selection 16 – DNA Research   22

    Selection 17 – Liberal Arts Education   23

    Selection 18 – Mount Everest   24

Answers and Explanations to PERT Reading Test 1   25

PERT Writing Test 1:

    Questions 1 to 5 – Rhetorical coherence, verb usage, subordination, tone   29

    Questions 6 to 10 – Pronoun usage, rhetorical function, citation, parallel structure, capitalization   31

    Questions 11 to 15 – Subject-verb agreement, concise restatement, pronoun usage, adverb usage, providing counterarguments   34

    Questions 16 to 20 – Rhetorical devices, placing sentences in correct order, commonly-confused words, combining sentences   37

    Questions 21 to 25 – Supporting your topic, providing arguments, pronoun-antecedent agreement, verse tense, cohesive devices   39

    Questions 26 to 30 – Clear pronoun reference, subordination and coordination, supporting your argument, parallel structure   41

Answers and Explanations to PERT Writing Test 1   43

PERT Reading Test 2:

    Selection 1 – The Mechanics of Motion   48

    Selection 2 – How to Bake a Cake   50

    Selection 3 – The Antarctic Ice Sheet   51

    Selection 4 – Don't Worry-Be Happy   52

    Selection 5 – The Theories of Jean Piaget   54

    Selection 6 – Stone Age Artists   56

    Selection 7 – Bad Service in the Service Industry   57

    Selection 8 – The Study of Philosophy   58

    Selection 9 – Abraham Lincoln   59

    Selection 10 – The Electron Microscope   60

    Selection 11 – Excerpt from *A Story of the Days to Come*   61

    Selection 12 – Excerpt from "Adoption of the Declaration of Human Rights"   62

    Selection 13 – The History of Polyphonic Music   63

    Selection 14 – Fast Food   64

Selection 15 – What Causes Cancer?	64
Selection 16 – Excerpt from *Oliver Twist*	65
Selection 17 – The HSBC Skyscraper	66
Selection 18 – The Input Hypothesis	66
Selection 19 – Measuring Brain Activity	67

Answers and Explanations to PERT Reading Test 2 — 69

PERT Writing Test 2:

- Questions 1 to 5 – Pronoun-antecedent agreement, modifier placement, parallel structure, rhetorical coherence and transitions — 74
- Questions 6 to 10 – Citation, rhetorical function, subject-verb agreement, revising and combining sentences — 76
- Questions 11 to 15 – Providing arguments, modifier placement, subordination, tone, capitalization — 79
- Questions 16 to 20 – Pronoun usage, concise restatement, providing counterarguments, commonly-confused words — 81
- Questions 21 to 25 – Placing sentences in correct order, clear pronoun reference, pronoun-antecedent agreement, providing arguments, capitalization — 83
- Questions 26 to 30 – Supporting your topic, subordination and coordination, taking effective notes, pronoun usage — 86

Answers and Explanations to PERT Writing Test 2 — 89

PERT Reading Test 3:

- Selection 1 – Archeological Excavation and Interpretation — 94
- Selection 2 – Reality TV and Celebrity Status — 96
- Selection 3 – Excerpt from "On Women's Right to Vote" — 97
- Selection 4 – Earthquakes — 98
- Selection 5 – The World's First Locomotive — 99
- Selection 6 – Research on Socioeconomic Inequality — 100
- Selection 7 – Wireless Technology and Social Media — 102

Selection 8 – Acid Rain ... 103

Selection 9 – Personality Theory ... 104

Selection 10 – Excerpt from *The Woman in White* ... 106

Selection 11 – The Rabies Vaccine ... 107

Selection 12 – The Giza Pyramids ... 108

Selection 13 – Excerpt from *Tess of the D'Ubervilles* ... 109

Selection 14 – Nutrition ... 110

Selection 15 – Vending Machines ... 111

Selection 16 – Lewis and Clark ... 112

Selection 17 – Skill Recall ... 113

Selection 18 – Excerpt from *Culture and Imperialism* ... 114

Answers and Explanations to PERT Reading Test 3 ... 115

PERT Writing Test 3:

Questions 1 to 5 – Rhetorical function, subject-verb agreement, commonly-confused words, paraphrasing, citation ... 119

Questions 6 to 10 – Capitalization, parallel structure, revising and combining sentences, supporting your argument, tone ... 123

Questions 11 to 15 – Misplaced modifiers, placing sentences in correct order, concise restatement, verb tense, coordination ... 126

Questions 16 to 20 – Parallel structure, providing counterarguments, modifier placement, subordination, clear pronoun reference ... 127

Questions 21 to 25 – Pronoun-antecedent agreement, providing arguments, restating, punctuation, verb tense and usage ... 129

Questions 26 to 30 – Subordination, supporting your topic, rhetorical coherence, capitalization, adjective usage ... 130

Answers and Explanations to PERT Writing Test 3 ... 134

PERT Test Format

The Florida Postsecondary Educational Readiness Test (PERT) is a college placement test that assesses your skills in reading, writing, and math. The PERT is a computer-adaptive test. This means that you will normally take the test on a computer, rather than on paper, and that your responses to previous questions will determine the difficulty level of subsequent questions. In other words, if you are answering the questions correctly, the problems should become more difficult as the test progresses. Questions on the PERT are multiple-choice.

Since the PERT is a secure test, the items in this book are not actual test questions. However, this practice material is designed to review the necessary skills covered on the exam by simulating the difficulty level and format of questions you may face on the actual test.

Please note that when you take the exam on the computer, you will see one selection, followed by one question, so certain selections may be repeated on the actual exam.

How to Use This Publication

On the following pages, you will see lists of the skill sets that are assessed on the PERT Reading and Writing Tests. The practice tests in this publication provide example questions for all of the reading and writing skill sets assessed on the actual test.

You should complete the first practice test especially carefully in order to become acquainted with the types of questions you will see on the PERT Reading and Writing Tests.

When you have completed practice test 1, study the answers and explanations in order to learn the how to solve the all of the types of questions on the PERT.

Pay special attention to the explanations that are provided after practice tests 2 and 3 as well since they also contain tips and strategies that you need for the exam.

PERT Reading Test Information and Tips

The PERT Reading Test has 30 questions. Only 25 of the questions will count towards your score.

You won't know which five questions aren't going to count, so do your best on each question.

There are various types of questions on the PERT Reading Test. The following list gives you an idea of the types of questions you may encounter on the actual exam.

- Determining the main idea of a selection
- Summarizing the key points from a selection
- Understanding specific points from a selection
- Stating them meaning of words or phrases as they are used in the context of the selection
- Analyzing the organizational structure of a selection
- Evaluating the function or purpose of a specific sentence within a selection
- Determining the purpose of the author in writing the selection
- Deciding which evidence best serves as an argument in favor of or against an assertion in the selection
- Ascertaining whether certain statements in the selection are unbiased facts or biased opinions
- Evaluating the reasoning and effectiveness of evidence provided in a selection
- Stating what ideas can be inferred or what conclusions can be drawn from a selection
- Determining the relationship between two sentences on a specific topic

- Understanding the relationships between and motivations of characters in fiction
- Assessing the tone of a selection
- Analyzing and comparing two texts with different styles

PERT Writing Test Information and Tips

Like the PERT Reading Test, the PERT Writing Test has 30 questions, but only 25 of them will count towards your final score.

When you take the PERT Writing Test, you will encounter some of the same selections that you will have seen on the reading section of the test. In order to simulate the actual testing experience, this publication also uses some of the reading selections in the writing practice tests.

Here is a list of the types of questions you may encounter on the PERT Writing Test:

- Establishing and supporting a topic or theme
- Using grammar, punctuation, and capitalization correctly:
    - Subject-verb agreement
    - Verb usage and tense
    - Pronoun-antecedent agreement
    - Avoiding unclear pronoun reference
    - Correct modifier placement
    - Coordination
    - Subordination
    - Parallel structure
    - Capitalization of proper nouns
- Providing arguments and counterarguments in a written selection
- Determining the appropriate tone to use in writing
- Restating and paraphrasing information from a selection
- Understanding how to cite information from a selection

- Recognizing commonly-confused words and making the correct word choice
- Expressing ideas clearly and concisely
- Ascertaining the correct order of sentences in a selection
- Synthesizing information from more than one sentence by effectively combining sentences
- Using transitional and cohesive devices correctly
- Understanding rhetorical coherence and identifying sentences that do not belong in a selection

The practice tests in this book contain all of the types of reading and writing questions listed above so that you will know what to expect on the day of your actual test.

PERT READING PRACTICE TEST 1

Read the selections and answer the questions that follow.

Teenage Smoking

Research funding is often devoted to the investigation of teenage smoking. Although studies reveal that smoking by adults has been declining steadily over the past few decades, the percentage of teenagers who smoke has only started to drop recently. In fact, the current statistics on this trend are really quite alarming because the rate of teenagers who smoke is nearly fifteen percent greater than the rate of adults who smoke.

Reasons for this trend include the phenomenon of peer pressure. Teenagers are generally more prone to pressure from their friends than adults, and smoking is one way to fit in with one's social group in order to achieve feelings of belonging. Further, with the increase in the use of social media and with many parents working long hours, some teenagers may feel lonely or socially alienated. Teenagers experiencing alienation are even more susceptible to fall into the trap of smoking because of peer pressure.

Recent research shows that the rise in teenage smoking in the last ten years has primarily taken place in youth from more affluent families, in other words, families in which both parents are working and earning good incomes. These new teenage smokers are not from disadvantaged homes, as most people seem to believe. Indeed, the facts demonstrate quite the opposite because the most striking and precipitous rise in smoking has been for teenagers from the most financially advantageous backgrounds.

Moreover, because of lawsuits against the major tobacco companies, the price of cigarettes has actually declined sharply over the past decade. The paradox is that the increased demand for cigarettes originated from new teenage smokers who are from well-off families. Yet, contrary to these market forces, the prices of some tobacco products have fallen during this time.

1) In the selection, the reference to "disadvantaged homes" provides:

    A.   a useful comparison.

    B.   evidence for the author's argument.

C. a dramatic shift in focus.

D. a rebuttal for a common fallacy.

2) What is the primary purpose of this selection?

A. to provide information on a recent trend

B. to emphasize the dangers of smoking

C. to dispel a common misconception

D. to highlight the difference between two types of teenagers

Ancient Cosmetics

The ancient Egyptians used eye shadow over 5,000 years ago. The cosmetic was used for personal beautification, as well as for practical reasons. Consisting of a paste made from malachite, a copper salt that was bright green, the eye paint protected against glare from the sun, in addition to being an attractive color. On her upper eye lids, Cleopatra wore blue eye shadow made of ground lapis lazuli stone, much like other women of her day.

The queen used the green malachite as an accent below her eyes, and kohl, which consisted of lead sulfide, to provide color to her eyelashes and eyebrows. Red ochre, iron-based clay, provided her with lip and cheek color. Henna, a reddish-brown dye that was derived from a bush, was also commonly used by women in those days as a nail polish. The henna was thickened with tannin from the bark or fruit of various trees in order to be suitable for cosmetic use. The use of this particular cosmetic was not limited to women. Men also used the substance to darken their hair and beards.

3) Which of the following words best describes the tone of this selection?

A. argumentative

B. persuasive

C. informative

D. condemning

The Function of the Actor

Hamlet said: "We end the heartache, and the thousand natural shocks that flesh is heir to." It has always been the function of the actor to be an emotional physician. He or she allows members of the audience to identify with the story and have feelings and sentiments that may have been difficult for them to experience otherwise.

The actor participates in a great tradition, so he or she must not be afraid to act as a mediator between the audience and their emotions. Acting is a challenging profession, and this has been the challenge of the actor since the beginning of time.

Inspiration is a creative tool of the actor. To be inspired is to be creative, and to be able to direct that creativity is the result of intelligence.

Accordingly, the duty of the serious actor is great. In ancient Greece thousands of years ago, acting served the same purpose that it still serves today. Its fundamental purpose has not changed from the time cave men lined up in a circle and performed their ritualistic chants and pantomimic dances to stir the emotions of their audience. Through these rituals, the primitive emotions were excited to a point of stimulation that propelled our civilization onward.

The Actor and the Audience

There has been a fundamental change in the relationship between the actor and the audience in recent years. According to Aristotelian principles, actors should provoke an emotional catharsis in the members of the audience. Traditionally, actors have provided this emotional release, but this is far from the case in many modern motion pictures and television programs. Many performances and productions nowadays lack gravitas; rather, they are based on contrived stories or weak plots that have been created merely as mindless diversions. When actors engage in such vacuous performances, they do not even begin to serve the higher purpose of their profession.

4) With which of the following ideas do both selections agree?

   A. Acting is a challenging profession.

   B. Modern acting has evolved to a higher level from traditional acting.

C. Actors often fail to provoke an emotional response from the audience.

D. Actors need to be intelligent in order to perform well.

The Power of Tornadoes

Tornadoes are one of the most severe types of weather phenomena. While many people fear tornadoes and their destructive power, few people understand their real causes and effects, nor are they aware of how to protect themselves from their devastating force.

Tornadoes, violently rotating columns of air, occur when a change in wind direction, coupled with an increase in wind speed, results in a spinning effect in the lower atmosphere. These whirling movements, which may not be visible to the naked eye, are exacerbated when the rotating air column shifts from a horizontal to a vertical position. As the revolving cloud draws in the warm air that surrounds it at ground level, its spinning motion begins to accelerate, thereby creating a funnel that extends from the cloud above it to the ground below. In this way, tornadoes become pendent from low pressure storm clouds.

When a tornado comes into contact with the ground, it produces a strong upward draft known as a vortex, a spiraling column of wind that can reach speeds in excess of 200 miles per hour. Traveling across the landscape, the tornado wreaks a path of concentrated destruction. It is not uncommon for these twisters to lift heavy objects, like cars or large animals, and throw them several miles. Houses that succumb to the force of the tornado seem to explode as the low air pressure inside the vortex collides with the normal air pressure inside the buildings.

Tornadoes can occur at any time of the year, but are typically most frequent during the summer months. Equally, tornadoes can happen at any time during the day, but usually occur between 3:00 in the afternoon and 9:00 in the evening. While these fierce funnels occur in many parts of the world, they are most common in the United States. On average, there are 1,200 tornadoes per year in this vast nation, causing 70 fatalities and 1,500 injuries.

Although taking myriad shapes and sizes, tornadoes are generally categorized as weak, strong, or violent. The majority of all tornadoes are classified as weak, meaning that their duration is less than 10 minutes, and they have a speed under 110 miles per hour. Comprising approximately 10 percent of all twisters, strong tornadoes may last for more than 20 minutes and reach speeds up to 205 miles per hour. Violent tornadoes are the rarest, occurring less than one percent of the time. While uncommon, tornadoes in this classification are the most devastating, lasting more than one hour and resulting in the greatest loss of life. Only violent tornadoes can completely destroy a well-built, solidly-constructed home, although weaker ones can also cause great damage.

5) Which of the following best describes the author's main purpose in the selection?

    A. to explain how tornadoes are classified

    B. to cast light on the causes and consequences of tornadoes

    C. to identify the most frequent type of tornadoes

    D. to demonstrate that tornadoes can result in fatalities

6) The selection implies that tornadoes are considered to be a severe weather phenomenon because:

    A. of the effects they create in the atmosphere.

    B. many people fear them.

    C. they produce strong vortexes.

    D. they can result in death and devastation.

7) All of the following key facts about tornadoes are mentioned in the selection except:

    A. the number of deaths from tornadoes.

    B. the time of day when tornadoes usually take place.

    C. the time of year when tornadoes are most common.

    D. the average wind speed of most tornadoes.

Marie Curie and the Discovery of Radium

Working in a run-down laboratory near Paris, Marie Curie worked around the clock to discover a radioactive element. When she finally captured her quarry in 1902, she named it "radium" after the Latin word meaning ray.

She had spent the day blending chemical compounds which could be used to destroy unhealthy cells in the body. As she was about to retire to bed that evening, she decided to return to her lab. There she found that the chemical compound had become crystalized in the bowls and was emitting the elusive light that she sought.

Inspired by the French scientist Henri Becquerel, Curie won the Nobel Prize for Chemistry in 1903. Upon winning the prize, she declared that the radioactive element would be used only to treat disease and would not be used for commercial profit.

Today radium provides the most effective remedy for certain types of cancer. Radium, now used for a treatment called radiotherapy, works by inundating diseased cells with radioactive particles. Its success lies in the fact that it eradicates malignant cells without any lasting ill effects on the body.

8) Which of the following is the best meaning of the word "quarry" as it is used in this selection?

    A. a precious commodity

    B. an unknown catalyst

    C. an object that is sought

    D. a chemical compound

9) Which of the following provides evidence for the author's belief that radium provides the most effective remedy for certain types of cancer?

    A. Radium is cost effective.

    B. Radium destroys cancerous cells.

    C. Radium has no long-term effects.

    D. Radium derives from a radioactive element.

Credit Card Spending

Credit card debt is a major cause of over one million bankruptcies each year. The reason is that many people get a credit card on impulse and fail to read the terms and conditions. By the time annual fees are accrued, payments can be missed, which causes balances to skyrocket.

Although we all would like to believe that credit card companies are culpable, individuals themselves are the real culprits. In short, if your credit card spending is out of control, the real cause of your financial mess is you.

If you can summon enough willpower and strength to manage your finances and spending, then you will find yourself the winner in the game of finance. It may be easy to get into debt, but getting out of debt is much more difficult.

One simple phrase sums up the solution to financial problems. If you don't have the money to spend, then don't spend it!

Personal Finance

It has to be said that external forces and market conditions have a huge impact on personal financial situations. Have you ever noticed that the things you buy at the store go up a few pennies between shopping trips? Not every week and not by much – just little by little – but they continue to creep up.

There is a way that the effect of price increases upon personal finances can be minimized: buy in quantity when prices are low. My philosophy is to set out to find the best prices I can get on quantity purchases of things such as bathroom items and dry and canned food, even if I have to use my credit card to get them. You will be surprised by how much you can save, for example, by buying a twenty pound bag of rice as opposed to a one pound bag.

10) The writer of selection 1 would disagree most strongly with which of the following statements from selection 2?

    A. External forces and market conditions have a huge impact on personal financial situations.

B. The things you buy at the store go up a few pennies between shopping trips.

C. There is a way that the effect of price increases upon personal finances can be minimized: buy in quantity when prices are low.

D. My philosophy is to set out to find the best prices I can get on quantity purchases of things such as bathroom items and dry and canned food, even if I have to use my credit card to get them.

Mount Rushmore in the Black Hills

In the Black Hills in the state of South Dakota, four visages protrude from the side of a mountain. The faces are those of four United States' presidents: George Washington, Thomas Jefferson, Theodore Roosevelt, and Abraham Lincoln. Overseen and directed by the Danish-American sculptor John Gutzon Borglum, the work on this giant display of outdoor art was a Herculean task that took 14 years to complete.

A South Dakota state historian named Doane Robinson originally conceived of the idea for the memorial sculpture. He proposed that the work be dedicated to popular figures, who were prominent in the western United States and accordingly suggested statues of western heroes such as Buffalo Bill Cody and Kit Carson. Deeming a project dedicated to popular heroes frivolous, Borglum rejected Robinson's proposal. It was Borglum's firm conviction that the mountain carving be used to memorialize individuals of national, rather than regional, importance.

Mount Rushmore therefore became a national memorial, dedicated to the four presidents who were considered most pivotal in US history. Washington was chosen on the basis of being the first president. Jefferson, who was of course a president, was also instrumental in the writing of the American Declaration of Independence. Lincoln was selected on the basis of the mettle he demonstrated during the American Civil War and Roosevelt for his development of Square Deal policy, as well as for being a proponent of the construction of the Panama Canal. Commencing with Washington's head first, Borglum quickly realized that it would be best to work on only one head at a time in order to make each one compatible with its surroundings. To help visualize the final outcome, he fashioned a 1.5 meter high plaster model on a scale of 1 to 12.

Work on the venture began in 1927 and was completed in 1941. The cost of the project was nearly one million dollars, which would be worth over seventy million dollars today. The financing for the project was provided mostly from national government funds and also from charitable donations from magnanimous and benevolent members of the public. The carving of the mountain was tedious and arduous work, employing 360 men who worked in groups of 30. Since occupational health and safety laws did not exist at that time, the daily working conditions on the mountainside could best be described as treacherous. For instance, men were often strapped inside leather harnesses that dangled over the cliff edge. Wearing these contraptions, workers needed great strength to withstand the exertion of drilling into the mountainside.

The workmen faced frequent delays due to a dearth of financial backing in the early days, in addition to inclement weather throughout the 14 year period. Adverse conditions were also discovered when the carving of Jefferson began. The detection of poor quality stone on the mountain to the left of Washington resulted in Jefferson's face being repositioned to the right side. A large amount of the rock had to be blasted away from the mountain using dynamite or pneumatic drills, and as a result, approximately 450,000 tons of rock still lies at the foot of the mountain today.

11) Why did Doane Robinson suggest that the western heroes be the subject of the monument?

   A. Western heroes were well-known and loved by the public.

   B. The westward expansion movement would not have been successful without Buffalo Bill Cody and Kit Carson.

   C. Such figures were of national import.

   D. The dedication of a sculpture to Western heroes would raise their profiles.

12) Which of the following statements accurately expresses the author's attitude about John Gutzon Borglum and his work?

   A. He was a talented and perceptive artist.

   B. He was profligate in his spending for the Mount Rushmore project.

C. He unnecessarily put his workmen at risk of accidents.

D. He was an incompetent craftsman.

Excerpt from *The Yellow Wallpaper*

One of those sprawling flamboyant patterns committing every artistic sin. It is dull enough to confuse the eye in following, pronounced enough to constantly irritate and provoke study, and when you follow the lame uncertain curves for a little distance they suddenly commit suicide—plunge off at outrageous angles, destroy themselves in unheard of contradictions.

The color is repellent, almost revolting; a smoldering unclean yellow, strangely faded by the slow-turning sunlight. It is a dull yet lurid orange in some places, a sickly sulfur tint in others. No wonder the children hated it! I should hate it myself if I had to live in this room long.

I suppose John never was nervous in his life. He laughs at me so about this wall-paper!

At first he meant to repaper the room, but afterwards he said that after the wall-paper was changed it would be the heavy bedstead, and then the barred windows, and then that gate at the head of the stairs, and so on.

"You know the place is doing you good," he said, "and really, dear, I don't care to renovate the house just for a three months' rental."

I wish I could get well faster. But I must not think about that. This paper looks to me as if it KNEW what a vicious influence it had!

13) When the narrator uses the word "it" in paragraph 1, she is referring to:

A. the room.

B. the gate.

C. the wallpaper.

D. the heavy bedstead.

14) From the selection, it can be inferred that the relationship between the narrator and her husband is:

   A. contented.
   B. strained.
   C. resigned.
   D. violent.

Computers and the Stock Market

The use of computers in the stock market helps to control national and international finance. These controls were originally designed in order to create long-term monetary stability and protect shareholders from catastrophic losses. Because of the high level of automation involved in buying and selling shares, computer-to-computer trading could now paradoxically result in a downturn in the stock market.

Such a slump in the market, if not properly regulated, could bring about a computer-led stock market crash. Needless to say, such an economic collapse would have disastrous consequences for the entire nation. For this reason, regulations have been put in place by NASDAQ, AMEX, and FTSE.

15) Which sentence best expresses the main idea of the selection?

   A. Regulations on computer-to-computer trading are considered to be a financial necessity.
   B. There are negative public views about regulations on computer-to-computer trading.
   C. NASDAQ, AMEX, and FTSE were initially opposed to establishing regulations on computer-to-computer trading.
   D. The role of computers in international markets has not been modified over time.

The Law of Perpetual Motion

Sentence 1: The law of perpetual motion states that objects in motion will remain in motion.

Sentence 2: Once a vehicle has gained momentum, it will stop only if the brakes are applied.

16) What does the second sentence do in relation to the first sentence?

    A. It applies the theory mentioned in the first sentence.

    B. It restates the theory mentioned in the first sentence.

    C. It gives a solution to the problem described in the first sentence.

    D. It contradicts the evidence provided in the first sentence.

Excerpt from the State v. Scopes Trial

Delivered by Ben G. McKenzie, 1925

This line of inquiry is wholly improper and argumentative. It is not a statement as to what the issues are. Your Honor has already held that this act is constitutional, it being the law of the land. There is but one issue before this court and jury, and that is, did the defendant violate the statute. If Your Honor would please consider that some of the witnesses in this case are not very well and others are awfully ignorant. Furthermore, we have just agreed among ourselves to disregard the so-called evidence and argue the case.

17) Within the selection, words such as "improper," "argumentative," and "ignorant" are used to support the speaker's intention to:

    A. placate the opposition.

    B. reconcile differing points of view.

    C. dispense with the current line of questioning.

    D. offer further evidence to support his argument.

Radioactive Waste

Highly concentrated radioactive waste is lethal and can remain so for thousands of years. Accordingly, the disposal of this material remains an issue in most energy-producing countries around the world. In the United States, for example, liquid forms of radioactive waste are usually stored in stainless steel tanks. For extra protection, the tanks are double-walled and surrounded by a concrete covering that is one meter thick. This storage solution is also utilized the United Kingdom, in most cases.

The long-term problem lies in the fact that nuclear waste generates heat as the radioactive atoms decay. This excess heat could ultimately result in a radioactive leak. Therefore, the liquid needs to be cooled by pumping cold water into coils inside the tanks. This means that the tanks are only a temporary storage solution. The answer to the long-term storage of nuclear waste may be fusing the waste into glass cylinders that are stored deep underground.

18) Which of the following assumptions has most influenced the writer?

    A. The threat of a radioactive leak is exaggerated by the public.

    B. The storage of radioactive waste in stainless steel tanks is extremely dangerous.

    C. The underground storage of glass cylinders containing radioactive waste is a very risky procedure.

    D. A radioactive leak would have disastrous consequences around the globe.

19) How are the tanks used for storing radioactive waste protected against leaks?

    A. They are encased in concrete.

    B. They contain waste only in liquid form.

    C. They provide a place where radioactive atoms can decay.

    D. The waste is stored in them only on a short-term basis.

Excerpt from *Robinson Crusoe*

I cannot say that after this, for five years, any extraordinary thing happened to me, but I lived on in the same course, in the same posture and place.

At last, being eager to view the circumference of my little kingdom, I resolved upon my cruise; and accordingly I victualed my ship for the voyage, putting in two dozen of loaves (cakes I should call them) of barley-bread, an earthen pot full of parched rice (a food I ate a good deal of), a little bottle of rum, half a goat, and powder and shot for killing more, and two large watch-coats, of those which, as I mentioned before, I had saved out of the seamen's chests; these I took, one to lie upon, and the other to cover me in the night.

It was the 6th of November, in the sixth year of my reign – or my captivity, which you please – that I set out on this voyage, and I found it much longer than I expected; having secured my boat, I took my gun and went on shore, climbing up a hill, which seemed to overlook that point where I saw the full extent of it, and resolved to venture. In my viewing the sea from that hill where I stood, I perceived a strong, and indeed a most furious current.

20) What does the narrator mean when he says that he "victualed" the ship for the voyage?

    A. He loaded hunting supplies.

    B. He packed clothing for the voyage.

    C. He put on food and edible supplies.

    D. He checked that he had bed clothes.

21) What is the narrator's tone when he states: "It was the 6th of November, in the sixth year of my reign"?

    A. sarcastic

    B. mournful

    C. factual

    D. sincere

Multiple Intelligences

(1) The theory of multiple intelligences is rapidly replacing the intelligence quotient, also known as IQ. (2) Long considered the only valid way of measuring intelligence, IQ is a less efficacious way to gauge intelligence since it reinforces many social and cultural stereotypes. (3) Recent psychometric research indicates that there has been a movement away from the IQ test, which is now seen as an indication of a person's academic ability. (4) The theory multiple intelligences is more useful than that of IQ because it measures practical skills such as spatial, visual, and musical ability.

(5) If a person has visual or spatial intelligence, he or she will be good at perceiving visual images. (6) To put it another way, people with spatial intelligence will have a knack for interpreting things like maps and charts and so on. (7) Verbal or linguistic intelligence is another one of the multiple intelligences, and it includes skills like public speaking or telling stories. (8) There is also musical intelligence, so for instance, if a person can sing or play a musical instrument, he or she probably possesses this type of intelligence. (9) Famous sports personalities have what is known as bodily or kinesthetic intelligence, which means that they are skilful in controlling their bodily movements. (10) If you ever have the occasion to teach someone with kinesthetic intelligence, you will quickly realize that trying to do so is the ultimate nightmare since sitting in a classroom for extended periods of time is definitely not something these types of learners enjoy.

(11) Howard Gardner, the researcher who designed the system of multiple intelligences, posits that while most people have one dominant type of intelligence, most of us have more than one type. (12) The theory of multiple intelligences therefore has implications for teaching and learning.

22) Which of the following sentences uses language that is unbiased?

    A. Sentence 2

    B. Sentence 4

    C. Sentence 10

    D. Sentence 11

23) Which of the following best contributes to the credibility of the information in the selection?

    A.   the use of academic vocabulary

    B.   the reference to recent psychometric research

    C.   the account of teaching someone with kinesthetic intelligence

    D.   the name of the researcher who designed the system of multiple intelligences

Michelangelo and the Sistine Chapel

(1) Michelangelo began work on the painting of the ceiling of the Sistine Chapel in the summer of 1508, assisted by six others who helped to mix his paint and plaster. (2) However, as work proceeded, the artist dismissed each of his assistants one by one, claiming that they lacked the competence necessary to do the task at hand.

(3) Described as the lonely genius, the painter himself often felt incompetent to complete the project entrusted to him by Pope Julius II. (4) Having trained as a sculptor, Michelangelo had an extremely low opinion of his own painting skills. (5) Yet, he went on to paint one of the most beautiful works in art history.

(6) In spite of his frequent personal misgivings, he persevered to paint the ceiling with his vision of the creation of the universe. (7) The nine scenes that he created ran in a straight line along the ceiling. (8) The scenes include the Separation of Light from Darkness, the Drunkenness of Noah, the Ancestors of Christ, and the Salvation of Mankind.

24) Which of the following sentences expresses an opinion of the author of the selection?

    A.   Sentence 2

    B.   Sentence 3

    C.   Sentence 4

    D.   Sentence 5

25) Why did Michelangelo dismiss his assistants?

    A. Because he decided that he preferred to mix his plaster by himself.

    B. Because their dismissal was requested by the Pope.

    C. Because he believed that they were inept craftsmen.

    D. Because they had no training in sculpture.

DNA Research

(1) The genetic characteristics of any organism are present in its DNA, which is the genetic material found in each and every living cell. (2) DNA is therefore a genetic code, and this genetic information is constructed from long molecules that appear to be in the shape of chains. (3) These DNA chains consist of four separate components called nucleotides.

(4) The order of these nucleotides on the DNA chain determines the genetic information for the cells. (5) Accordingly, the specific genetic information on any point of this DNA chain will determine a particular genetic trait. (6) On an individual level, a particular portion of your DNA might show your doctor if you are susceptible to a disease, like cancer or Alzheimer's.

(7) In order to carry out what is known as genetic engineering, gene splicing needs to be done first. (8) Gene splicing, the process whereby a small part of the DNA of one organism is removed and inserted into the DNA chain of another organism, has produced results like the super tomato. (9) When creating the super tomato, scientists isolated the gene resistant to cold temperatures on the DNA chain of a particular type of cold-water fish, removed it, and inserted it into an ordinary tomato plant. (10) This resulted in a new type of tomato plant that can thrive in cold weather conditions.

(11) However, gene splicing has become controversial lately. (12) As animal rights groups have come more into prominence socially and politically, and people are more and more aware of the suffering of animals, many people question whether using animals in this way is medically reasonable, or whether it is even ethical or moral.

26) From this selection, it seems safe to conclude that:

    A. the super tomato was the first case of gene splicing.

B. the super tomato is only one example of gene splicing.

C. DNA from tomatoes has also been inserted into certain types of fish.

D. the interests of animal rights groups will soon fade from the public eye.

27) In the selection, sentence 6:

A. provides an example that supports sentence 5.

B. gives a paraphrase in order to restate sentence 5.

C. refutes the evidence stated in sentence 5.

D. uses a subtlety to reinterpret sentence 5.

Liberal Arts Education

The notion of liberal arts education is believed to have been established in ancient Greece. Including the disciplines of logic, rhetoric, and grammar, a liberal arts education in those days was designed to train members of society to undertake important civic duties, such as jury service and public debate. In modern parlance, the term "liberal arts education" can be interpreted in a variety of ways, although it is generally taken to mean that the studies will include courses in one or more of the subject areas of the humanities, such as languages, literature, or philosophy.

28) The best definition of the word "parlance" as it is used in the selection is:

A. style of speaking

B. everyday language

C. debate

D. etiquette

Mount Everest

Since its discovery in 1749, Mount Everest was unquestionably considered to be the world's highest mountain. However, in 1986 George Wallerstein from the University of Washington posited that another Himalayan mountain, named K-2, was higher than Everest. It took an expedition of Italian scientists, who used a surfeit of technological devices, to disprove Wallerstein's claim.

29) Which of the following search terms would be best used in a search engine on the Internet in order to locate the information contained in the selection?

    A. George Wallerstein K-2

    B. How High is Mount Everest

    C. Discovery of Mount Everest

    D. Himalayan Mountains

30) According to the selection, which one of the following statements is correct?

    A. Since 1749, Mount Everest has universally been considered to be the tallest mountain in the world.

    B. Wallerstein fell into disrepute in the academic community after his claims were disproved.

    C. Using technological equipment, Italian scientists refuted Wallerstein's hypothesis.

    D. The University of Washington fully supported Wallerstein's claims about K-2.

PERT PRACTICE TEST 1 – ANSWERS AND EXPLANATIONS

1) The correct answer is D. The test states that "new teenage smokers are not from disadvantaged homes, as most people seem to believe." The phrase "as most people seem to believe" indicates that a common fallacy (or misbelief) is being rebutted (or disproved).

2) The correct answer is A. The primary purpose of this selection is to provide information on a recent trend. The main purpose is provided in the last sentence of the first paragraph, which states: "In fact, the current statistics on this trend are really quite alarming because the rate of teenagers who smoke is nearly fifteen percent greater than the rate of adults who smoke."

3) The correct answer is C. The selection focuses on historical facts, such as Cleopatra's use of cosmetics and the history of the cosmetic use of henna. Thus, the selection is informative in nature.

4) The correct answer is A. The author of selection 1 states in paragraph 2 that "acting is a challenging profession." The author of selection 2 implies that acting is challenging because he talks about recent changes in the acting profession, as well as the fact that acting should serve a higher purpose.

5) The correct answer is B. Remember that the main idea of the selection will often be stated in the first paragraph. In our selection, the first paragraph states: "few people understand their real causes and effects, nor are they aware of how to protect themselves from their devastating force." The phrase "causes and effects" indicates that the author wishes to cast light on the causes and consequences of tornadoes.

6) The correct answer is D. Tornadoes are considered to be a severe weather phenomenon because they can result in death and devastation. The selection discusses the damage to property from tornadoes, as well as stating the number of fatalities and injuries caused by tornadoes.

7) The correct answer is D. The selection mentions the various wind speeds of the different categories of tornadoes, but it does not provide an average wind speed.

8) The correct answer is C. For vocabulary questions like this one, look for synonyms in the selection. In sentence one, we see the word "discover." In the last sentence of paragraph two,

we see the phrase "the elusive light that she sought." Therefore, we can surmise that "quarry" is something one wants to discover or an object being sought.

9) The correct answer is B. Be careful. Questions like this will have distractor answers. In other words, they will reiterate phrases from the selection, although these phrases do not answer the question. We know that answer B is correct because the final sentence of the selection states: "Its success lies in the fact that it eradicates malignant cells without any lasting ill effects on the body." You may be tempted to choose answer C. However, answer C is too general since radium has long-term positive effects [i.e., destroying malignant cells] without having any long-term negative effects.

10) The correct answer is D. The writer of selection 1 speaks out against credit card debt, so she would disagree with the following statement from selection 2: "My philosophy is to set out to find the best prices I can get on quantity purchases of things such as bathroom items and dry and canned food, even if I have to use my credit card to get them."

11) The correct answer is A. Doane Robinson suggested that Western heroes be the subject of Mount Rushmore because they were well-known and loved by the public. In paragraph 2, we see that Robinson described these men as "popular figures."

12) The correct answer is A. The author's attitude about John Gutzon Borglum and his work is that Borglum was a talented and perceptive artist. Paragraph 2 explains Borglum's perception in wanting to memorialize individuals of national import, while paragraph 3 describes the artist's meticulous work practices.

13) The correct answer is C. We know that the narrator is talking about the wallpaper because she is describing the patterns on the paper. She then goes on to talk about the wallpaper in the majority of the selection.

14) The correct answer is B. The selection mentions various ways in which the narrator's husband will not accommodate her wishes, so the reader can assume that their relationship is difficult or strained.

15) The correct answer is A. The selection states that "computer-to-computer trading could result in a downturn in the stock market." Further, this downturn could result in a "computer-led stock market crash." In order to avoid these negative results, the regulations are needed.

Answers B and C are not stated in the selection. Answer D is incorrect because the selection talks about how the use of computers has changed over time.

16) The correct answer is A. The second sentence deals with only one vehicle, not all objects. So, the second sentence applies the rule mentioned in the first sentence to one specific situation. Therefore, we cannot say that the sentences restate the same idea.

17) The correct answer is C. The speaker uses the words "improper," "argumentative," and "ignorant" to dispense with the current line of questioning. In other words, he is asserting that there should be no further discussion of the issues of the case. The selection tells us that the judge has ruled that the evidence be disregarded, so we know that the speaker is not offering further evidence.

18) The correct answer is D. The author implies that a radioactive leak would have dire consequences since he opens the selection with this sentence: "Highly concentrated radioactive waste is lethal and can remain so for thousands of years."

19) The correct answer is A. The tanks are protected against leaks because they are encased in concrete. The fourth sentence of paragraph one states: "For extra protection, the tanks are double-walled and surrounded by a concrete covering that is one meter thick."

20) The correct answer is C. "Victual" is an antiquated word meaning food. We can understand this from the context of the selection because the narrator talks about putting bread, rice, and meat on the ship.

21) The correct answer is A. The narrator is being sarcastic. He is stranded and alone, so there is no one over whom he can reign.

22) The correct answer is D. Words or phrases that express an opinion are known as biased language. Unbiased language means that the information is factual and impartial, rather than being based on opinion. The words "efficacious" from sentence 2, "more useful" from sentence 4, and "ultimate nightmare" from sentence 10 are biased language.

23) The correct answer is D. The name of a particular researcher is more credible than reference to research studies in general. Note that vocabulary and personal anecdotes, as stated in answers A and C, do not usually add to the credibility of information in a selection.

24) The correct answer is D. The following sentence expresses an opinion of the author rather than a fact: "Yet, he went on to paint one of the most beautiful works in art history." The adjectival phrase "the most beautiful" indicates that an opinion is being given.

25) The correct answer is C. Michelangelo dismissed his assistants because he believed that they were inept craftsmen. See the last sentence of paragraph 1, which states that "as work proceeded, the artist dismissed each of his assistants one by one, claiming that they lacked the competence necessary to do the task at hand."

26) The correct answer is B. The phrase "results like the super tomato" indicates that the super tomato is only one example. The other ideas are not implied by the selection.

27) The correct answer is A. Sentence 6 provides an example because it uses the phrases "on an individual level" and "like cancer."

28) The correct answer is B. The selection talks about how the word "parlance" can be interpreted, so we know that we are offering a paraphrase of the word in everyday language

29) The correct answer is A. The majority of the selection talks about George Wallerstein's K-2 hypothesis. The first sentence serves as a general introduction to the main theme of the selection.

30) The correct answer is C. The Italian team confirmed that Everest was, in fact, the tallest mountain in the world. This answer is supported by the last sentence in the selection, which states: "It took an expedition of Italian scientists, who used a surfeit of technological devices, to disprove Wallerstein's claim."

PERT WRITING PRACTICE TEST 1

Read the selection below and then answer the questions.

The Pilgrims

(1) A group of English separatists known as the Pilgrims left England to live in Amsterdam in 1608. (2) After spending a few years in their new city, however, many members of the group felt that they did not have enough independence. (3) In 1617, the Pilgrims decided to leave Amsterdam to immigrate to America.

(4) Due to their lack of social standing, they had many financial problems that prevented them from beginning the journey. (5) Their inability to finance themselves caused many disputes and disagreements. (6) The Pilgrims finally managed to resolve these conflicts when they obtained financing from a well-known and respected London businessman named Thomas Weston. (7) The famous writer Samuel Pepys also lived in London at that time.

(8) Having secured Weston's monetary support, the group returned to England to pick up some additional passengers. (9) After 65 days at sea, the Pilgrims reached America in December, 1620. (10) While the early days of their new lives were filled with hope and promise, the harsh winter proved to be too much for some of the settlers. (11) Nearly half of the Pilgrims died during that first winter.

1) Which sentence does NOT belong in the selection?

    A. Sentence 4

    B. Sentence 5

    C. Sentence 7

    D. Sentence 10

2) Which of the following sentences would the author most likely use to continue the selection?

    A. It was such a pity that this happened.

    B. Yet, those who lived went on to work hard and prosper.

C. That is why the Pilgrims play such a crucial role in US history.

D. Accordingly, they were buried in a local cemetery that has become a historical landmark.

3) Choose the word or words that best complete the sentence.

Never in my life _____ such a beautiful sight.

A. have I seen

B. I have seen

C. did I see

D. I had saw

4) Which of the following sentences is incorrect?

A. I was going to studying this evening, but the noise next door made it impossible.

B. I was going to studying this evening; however, the noise next door made it impossible.

C. I was going to studying this evening, however, the noise next door made it impossible.

D. I was going to studying this evening. However, the noise next door made it impossible.

5) Read the selection below and then answer the question.

Due to health issues, you are going to email your professor to ask for an extension of time to complete your research paper. Which of the following would be the best tone to use?

A. deferential

B. assertive

C. informal

D. guarded

6) Choose the word or words that best complete the sentence.

She was hoping to buy a new car _____ would be spacious enough to transport her equipment.

A. it

B. one which

C. one

D. which

Read the selection below and then answer the question.

Multiple Intelligences

(1) The theory of multiple intelligences is rapidly replacing the intelligence quotient, also known as IQ. (2) Long considered the only valid way of measuring intelligence, IQ is a less efficacious way to gauge intelligence since it reinforces many social and cultural stereotypes. (3) Recent psychometric research indicates that there has been a movement away from the IQ test, which is now seen as an indication of a person's academic ability. (4) The theory multiple intelligences is more useful than that of IQ because it measures practical skills such as spatial, visual, and musical ability.

(5) If a person has visual or spatial intelligence, he or she will be good at perceiving visual images. (6) To put it another way, people with spatial intelligence will have a knack for interpreting things like maps and charts and so on. (7) Verbal or linguistic intelligence is another one of the multiple intelligences, and it includes skills like public speaking or telling stories. (8) There is also musical intelligence, so if, for instance, a person can sing or play a musical instrument, he or she probably possesses this type of intelligence. (9) Famous sports personalities have what is known as bodily or kinesthetic intelligence, which means that they are skilful in controlling their bodily movements. (10) If you ever have the occasion to teach someone with kinesthetic intelligence, you will quickly realize that trying to do so is the ultimate

nightmare since sitting in a classroom for extended periods of time is definitely not something these types of learners enjoy.

(11) Howard Gardner, the researcher who designed the system of multiple intelligences, posits that while most people have one dominant type of intelligence, <u>most of us have more than one type</u>. (12) The theory of multiple intelligences therefore has implications for teaching and learning.

7) The author of the selection uses the underlined phrase in order to:

    A.   refute the theory of multiple intelligences.

    B.   transition to her final assertion.

    C.   introduce a new point.

    D.   paraphrase the previous sentence.

Read the selection below and then answer the question.

DNA Research

(1) The genetic characteristics of any organism are present in its DNA, which is the genetic material found in each and every living cell. (2) DNA is therefore a genetic code, and this genetic information is constructed from long molecules that appear to be in the shape of chains. (3) These DNA chains consist of four separate components called nucleotides.

(4) The order of these nucleotides on the DNA chain determines the genetic information for the cells. (5) Accordingly, the specific genetic information on any point of this DNA chain will determine a particular genetic trait. (6) On an individual level, a particular portion of your DNA might show your doctor if you are susceptible to a disease, like cancer or Alzheimer's.

(7) In order to carry out what is known as genetic engineering, gene splicing needs to be done first. (8) Gene splicing, the process whereby a small part of the DNA of one organism is removed and inserted into the DNA chain of another organism, has produced results like the super tomato. (9) When creating the super tomato, scientists isolated the gene resistant to cold temperatures on the DNA chain of a particular type of cold-water fish, removed it, and inserted it

into an ordinary tomato plant. (10) This resulted in a new type of tomato plant that can thrive in cold weather conditions.

(11) However, gene splicing has become controversial lately. (12) As animal rights groups have come more into prominence socially and politically, and people are more and more aware of the suffering of animals, many people question whether using animals in this way is medically reasonable, or whether it is even ethical or moral.

8) Which of the following sentences demonstrates the best way to cite the information in sentence 12?

    A. It has been questioned whether using animals for medical research is reasonable.

    B. Recent research indicates that "animal rights groups question whether the suffering of animals for medical reasons is ethical or moral."

    C. According to *DNA Research,* more and more people are questioning whether using animals for DNA research is "medically reasonable."

    D. Many people have doubts about whether using animals for DNA research is "medically reasonable, or whether it is even ethical or moral" (*DNA Research*).

9) Which of the following sentences uses correct parallel structure?

    A. The vacation was fun, exciting, and gave me a great chance to unwind.

    B. I went jet skiing, surfing, and also snorkeled for the first time on our vacation.

    C. The hotel was elegant, comfortable, and the staff members were so friendly.

    D. I enjoyed our hotel room, relaxed in the spa, and ate some truly delicious, well-balanced meals on our vacation.

10) Read the sentence that follows. Then choose the part that needs capitalization.

(A) My mom and I went to see (B) yellowstone park (C) with my aunt (D) in the spring last year.

   A.   Part A

   B.   Part B

   C.   Part C

   D.   Part D

11) Which one of the following sentences has correct subject-verb agreement?

   A.   The knives or the forks goes into that drawer.

   B.   Neither Marisa nor Amy are home.

   C.   Each of the men is very strong and determined.

   D.   Every one of the books are on the shelf.

12) Read the sentence and answer the question.

They told me that I would pass my driving test, but I didn't believe it.

Which of the following sentences is the <u>best</u> revision of the one above?

   A.   I knew I wouldn't pass my driving test.

   B.   I doubted whether I would pass my driving test.

   C.   I was skeptical about my driving test.

   D.   The result of my driving test was dubious.

13) Choose the sentence that is written correctly.

   A.   Who did the interview panel select for the job?

   B.   Whom did the interview panel select for the job?

   C.   Who the interview panel selected for the job?

   D.   Whom the interview panel selected for the job?

14) What is the best replacement for the underlined words in the following sentence?

The teacher asked me to speak up because she could not hear me.

- A. speak more loudly
- B. speak more louder
- C. speak more loud
- D. speak louder

15) Read the selection below and then answer the question.

After the college made attendance at evening classes optional, the number of absences from evening classes increased. Therefore, attendance at evening classes should be made mandatory once again.

Which of the following is the best counterargument to the selection?

- A. Attendance at evening classes is never going to increase because students detest having classes at that time of day.
- B. It is very difficult to concentrate during the evening hours, so evening classes should be dropped altogether.
- C. There may have been other factors that influenced the decline in attendance at evening classes, other than the attendance policy having been changed.
- D. Attending evening classes is important because it instills self-discipline in students.

Read the selection below and then answer the question.

Mount Rushmore in the Black Hills

In the Black Hills in the state of South Dakota, four visages protrude from the side of a mountain. The faces are those of four United States' presidents: George Washington, Thomas Jefferson, Theodore Roosevelt, and Abraham Lincoln. Overseen and directed by the Danish-

American sculptor John Gutzon Borglum, the work on this giant display of outdoor art was a Herculean task that took 14 years to complete.

A South Dakota state historian named Doane Robinson originally conceived of the idea for the memorial sculpture. He proposed that the work be dedicated to popular figures, who were prominent in the western United States and accordingly suggested statues of western heroes such as Buffalo Bill Cody and Kit Carson. Deeming a project dedicated to popular heroes frivolous, Borglum rejected Robinson's proposal. It was Borglum's firm conviction that the mountain carving be used to memorialize individuals of national, rather than regional, importance.

Mount Rushmore therefore became a national memorial, dedicated to the four presidents who were considered most pivotal in US history. Washington was chosen on the basis of being the first president. Jefferson, who was of course a president, was also instrumental in the writing of the American Declaration of Independence. Lincoln was selected on the basis of the mettle he demonstrated during the American Civil War and Roosevelt for his development of Square Deal policy, as well as for being a proponent of the construction of the Panama Canal. Commencing with Washington's head first, Borglum quickly realized that it would be best to work on only one head at a time in order to make each one compatible with its surroundings. To help visualize the final outcome, he fashioned a 1.5 meter high plaster model on a scale of 1 to 12.

Work on the venture began in 1927 and was completed in 1941. The cost of the project was nearly one million dollars, which would be worth over seventy million dollars today. The financing for the project was provided mostly from national government funds and also from charitable donations from magnanimous and benevolent members of the public. The carving of the mountain was tedious and arduous work, employing 360 men who worked in groups of 30. Since occupational health and safety laws did not exist at that time, the daily working conditions on the mountainside could best be described as treacherous. For instance, men were often strapped inside leather harnesses that dangled over the cliff edge. Wearing these contraptions, workers needed great strength to withstand the exertion of drilling into the mountainside.

The workmen faced frequent delays due to a dearth of financial backing in the early days, in addition to inclement weather throughout the 14 year period. Adverse conditions were also discovered when the carving of Jefferson began. The detection of poor quality stone on the mountain to the left of Washington resulted in Jefferson's face being repositioned to the right side. A large amount of the rock had to be blasted away from the mountain using dynamite or pneumatic drills, and as a result, approximately 450,000 tons of rock still lies at the foot of the mountain today.

16) Which of the following sentences most clearly describes when work on Mount Rushmore was completed?

    A.   Work on Mount Rushmore was completely relatively recently.

    B.   Work on Mount Rushmore was completed in the middle of the nineteenth century.

    C.   Work on Mount Rushmore was completed many years ago.

    D.   Work on Mount Rushmore was completed around the mid-1900s.

17) Choose the word or words that best completes the sentence.

He lost his scholarship _____ a consequence of his poor grades.

    A.   because of

    B.   as

    C.   since

    D.   due to

18) Choose the best order for the following sentences.

    1)   Genova, who has a PhD in neuroscience from Harvard, has become a *New York Times* best-selling author.

    2)   Published in 2009, *Still Alice* is a novel by Lisa Genova.

    3)   The book's success lies in its credible depiction of one woman's struggle with early-onset Alzheimer's disease.

4) The book's vivid representation of Alice's descent into forgetfulness and confusion also contributes to its appeal with readers.

    A.   2, 1, 3, 4

    B.   1, 3, 4, 2

    C.   2, 1, 4, 3

    D.   2, 4, 3, 1

19) Which of the following sentences uses the underlined word correctly?

    A.   Failure to study will <u>effect</u> your grades.

    B.   A scientific <u>principal</u> is a concise mathematical statement about the relationship of one object to another.

    C.   The run-away thief <u>eluded</u> the police officer.

    D.   He thought he saw an oasis in the desert, but it was an optical <u>allusion</u>.

20) Which is the best way to combine the two following sentences?

She worked on her presentation all night in order to be sure that her case was compelling.

Her audience was discerning and needed to be persuaded about the efficacy of her proposal.

    A.   She worked on her presentation all night in order to be sure that her case was compelling, but her audience was discerning needed to be persuaded about the efficacy of her proposal.

    B.   She worked on her presentation all night in order to be sure that her case was compelling; moreover, her audience was discerning needed to be persuaded about the efficacy of her proposal.

C. Due to the fact that her audience was discerning needed to be persuaded about the efficacy of her proposal, she worked on her presentation all night in order to be sure that her case was compelling.

D. She worked on her presentation all night because her case was compelling and so that her discerning audience could be persuaded.

Read the selection below and then answer the questions that follow.

Radioactive Waste

Highly concentrated radioactive waste is lethal and can remain so for thousands of years. Accordingly, the disposal of this material remains an issue in most energy-producing countries around the world. In the United States, for example, liquid forms of radioactive waste are usually stored in stainless steel tanks. For extra protection, the tanks are double-walled and surrounded by a concrete covering that is one meter thick. This storage solution is also utilized the United Kingdom, in most cases.

The long-term problem lies in the fact that nuclear waste generates heat as the radioactive atoms decay. This excess heat could ultimately result in a radioactive leak. Therefore, the liquid needs to be cooled by pumping cold water into coils inside the tanks. This means that the tanks are only a temporary storage solution. The answer to the long-term storage of nuclear waste may be fusing the waste into glass cylinders that are stored deep underground.

21) Which of the following sentences would the author most likely use to continue the selection?

A. Only time will tell whether storing glass cylinders underground is a viable long-term solution.

B. If that does not work, there are likely to be a number of other options.

C. Underground storage has also been attempted in other countries.

D. Therefore, the long-term storage of nuclear waste is a highly volatile process.

22) Which of the following details from the selection would best support an argument against any long-term storage of radioactive waste?

- A. This excess heat could ultimately result in a radioactive leak.
- B. Therefore, the liquid needs to be cooled by pumping cold water into coils inside the tanks.
- C. This means that the tanks are only a temporary storage solution.
- D. The answer to the long-term storage of nuclear waste may be fusing the waste into glass cylinders that are stored deep underground.

23) Which of the following sentences is written correctly?

- A. The group lost their enthusiasm for the project.
- B. The class hopes to elect Shanika as its representative.
- C. A student needs to study hard in order to pass their final exams.
- D. If my friends need anything, he or she can call me anytime.

24) Choose the word or words that best complete the sentence.

While snow showers _____ normally common in the north during the winter, precipitation is unlikely tomorrow.

- A. would be
- B. will be
- C. being
- D. are

25) Which of the following sentences is incorrect?

- A. Because it is warm all year round, Florida has many out-of-state visitors during December.

B. Due to being warm all year round, Florida has many out-of-state visitors during December.

C. Warm all year round, Florida has many out-of-state visitors during December.

D. Florida has many out-of-state visitors during December, in spite of warmth all year round.

26) Which of the following sentences uses clear pronouns?

A. Although Terry had a fight with his brother, he was not hurt.

B. They should not have made a law against parking here if it is not going to be enforced.

C. Many people go to see the cherry blossoms in Washington, which is really beautiful.

D. All of my family members bought me birthday presents, even though I had told them not to.

27) Which of the following sentences is incorrect?

A. Tom is highly intelligent, and so is his younger brother.

B. Tom is highly intelligent, just like his younger brother.

C. Tom is highly intelligent, and in the same way is his younger brother.

D. Like his younger brother, Tom is highly intelligent.

28) Imagine that you are writing a paper that argues that only children often suffer from loneliness when they are growing up.

Which of the following sources of evidence would least support your argument?

A. Interviews with only children.

B. Quotations from famous people who grew up in large families.

- C. Reference to recent research that describes the emotional aspects of loneliness.
- D. A quotation from an eminent psychologist who has worked with only children.

29) Which of the following sentences uses correct parallel structure?

- A. My brother likes to tell stories as well as reading.
- B. My car was damaged on the hood, fender, and on the bumper.
- C. She brought along cookies, as well as cake.
- D. My mother, friend, and the neighbor congratulated me on passing the exam.

30) Choose the word or words that best complete the sentence.

I bought my friends _____ favorite food and snacks for the party.

- A. their
- B. there
- C. they're
- D. their'

PERT WRITING PRACTICE TEST 1 – ANSWERS AND EXPLANATIONS

1) The correct answer is C. Samuel Pepys was a writer who had no relationship with the Pilgrims, so this sentence is irrelevant and does not belong in the selection.

2) The correct answer is B. In the last paragraph of the selection, the writer states that "the early days of their new lives were filled with hope and promise." This is a positive statement about the lives of the Pilgrims. In order to end the selection on a similar positive note, the writer would therefore likely continue as follows: "Yet, those who lived went on to work hard and prosper."

3) The correct answer is A. This question is an example of the inverted sentence structure. When a sentence begins with a negative phrase [no sooner, not only, never, etc.], the present perfect tense [have + past participle] can be used. In addition, the auxiliary verb "have" must be placed in front of the grammatical subject of the sentence [I]. The sentence begins with the word "never," so the auxiliary very "have" needs to be place before the subject of the sentence ("I") and the main verb ("seen").

4) The correct answer is C. In other words, sentence C is the incorrect sentence. The word "however" is a sentence linker. As such, it can be used at the beginning of a sentence to link to the idea contained in the previous sentence. Sentence linkers need to be followed by a comma and preceded by a period or semicolon, so sentences B and D are correct. The word "but" is a subordinator. Subordinators need to be preceded by a comma, so sentence A is correct as written.

5) The correct answer is A. For questions about tone, think carefully about the situation. If you are going to ask your professor for an extension of time for whatever reason, you need to show respect for his or her decision. "Deferential" means respectful, so A is the correct answer.

6) The correct answer is D. The word "which" forms a relative clause that describes the car she is hoping to purchase. The other options are not grammatically correct.

7) The correct answer is B. The author emphasizes the plural nature of multiple intelligence by stating in this sentence that "most of us have more than one type" of intelligence. She reiterates the multiple nature of intelligence to transition to the point about teaching and learning that she makes in the last sentence of the selection.

8) The correct answer is D. For questions like this one that are asking you about appropriate citation techniques, remember that the title of the selection needs to be stated at the beginning

of the sentence or in parentheses at the end of the sentence. For this reason, answers A and B are incorrect. Also remember that the information needs to be in quotation marks where two or more exact words are being quoted from the selection. Finally, the citation needs to reflect the information from the selection correctly. Answer C does not include any reference to the ethical and moral considerations, so it is not a full paraphrase of what is stated in the selection. For these reasons, Answer D is the best answer.

9) The correct answer is D. This question is about correct parallel structure, also known as parallelism. In order to follow the grammatical rules of parallelism, you must be sure that all of the items you give in a series are of the same part of speech. So, all of the items must be nouns or verbs, for example. In other words, you should not use both nouns and verbs in a list. Where verbs are used, they should be in the same tense. In sentence D, the words "enjoyed," "relaxed," and "ate" are all verbs in the past tense. Sentence A incorrectly uses adjectives ("fun" and "exciting") and verbs ("gave"), while sentence B mixes the –ing and –ed verb forms. Sentence C mixes adjectives ("elegant" and "comfortable") with nouns ("staff members").

10) The correct answer is B. Yellowstone Park is a proper noun, which is a name for a person, place, or organization, so the "y" and the "p" need to be capitalized. References to family members are not capitalized when used with the pronoun "my." The names of seasons are also not capitalized.

11) The correct answer is C. For questions on subject-verb agreement, you need to be sure to use a singular verb with a singular subject and a plural verb with a plural subject. While this sounds straightforward, complications can arise with certain words like "each," "every," "neither," and "either," all of which are in fact singular.

12) The correct answer is B. Restatement questions like this are asking you to find a word that can be used to restate a phrase from the original sentence. The idea "I didn't believe it" from the first sentence is best restated by the word "doubted" in answer choice B. Note that answer C is not the best answer because your skepticism is about passing the test, not about the test in general.

13) The correct answer is B. This question tests your knowledge of "who" and "whom." Remember to use "who" when the person you are talking about is doing the action, but to use "whom" when the person is receiving an action. In this sentence, the candidate is receiving the

action of being selected. So, the question should begin with "whom." The auxiliary verb "did" needs to come directly after "whom" to have the correct word order for this type of question.

14) The correct answer is A. The word "speak" is a verb, so it needs to be used with the adverb "loudly." The other answer choices are not grammatically correct.

15) The correct answer is C. When a question asks you for a counterargument, you need to ask yourself what situation or evidence would cast doubt on the assertion made in the selection. In this question, the selection is asserting that attendance should be made mandatory due to the increase in absences. Bringing up other factors that may have influenced the attendance would cast doubt on the assertion since the assertion implies that the increase in absences is solely attributable to the change in the attendance policy.

16) The correct answer is D. For questions like this one, you need to find the answer that is as specific as possible. We know from paragraph 4 of the selection that Mount Rushmore was completed in 1941. The answer that most closely paraphrases this idea is answer D, which states that the monument was finished "around the mid-1900s."

17) The correct answer is B. The word "as" is needed in order to complete the colloquial phrase "as a consequence of." The other answer choices are not grammatically correct.

18) The correct answer is A. When you have to put sentences in the correct order in questions like this one, you should first focus on the chronological sequence of events. Then look at the pronouns and linking words that are used to create coherence and flow between the sentences in the selection. We know that we have to begin with sentence 2 because it provides the first mention of the title of the book, as well as the author's name and the year of publication. Sentence 1 connects to the author's name in sentence 2. Sentence 3 then links the idea of the book's success back to the fact that the book is a best-seller from sentence 1. Finally, sentence 4 links the word "representation" back to the word "depiction" in sentence 3. So, the correct order of the sentences is 2, 1, 3, 4.

19) The correct answer is C. There will certainly be questions on commonly-confused words on the exam. Sentence A confuses the word "affect" with "effect," while sentence B confuses "principal" and "principle." Finally, sentence D confuses "allusion" with "illusion." "Elude" is used correctly in sentence C, but be careful not to confuse it with "allude."

20) The correct answer is C. For questions asking you to combine two sentences, look to see whether there is a cause and effect relationship between the two sentences. In this question, the woman works so hard on her presentation because she needs to persuade the audience. Sentence C is the only sentence that expresses this cause and effect relationship correctly.

21) The correct answer is A. The previous sentences in the paragraph talk about long-term solutions and whether they will be effective. Sentence A sums up the paragraph because it uses the phrase "viable long-term solution."

22) The correct answer is A. Remember that when a question asks you for a counterargument, you need to ask yourself what situation or evidence would cast doubt on the primary assertion made in the selection. In this selection, we are talking about safe storage solutions for radioactive waste. The idea that there would be a leak brings to light an extremely unsafe outcome of waste storage, so A is the best answer.

23) The correct answer is B. This question is asking you about pronoun-antecedent agreement. Pronouns are words like the following: he, she, it, they, and them. An antecedent is a phrase that precedes the pronoun in the sentence. Pronouns must agree with their antecedents, so use singular pronouns with singular antecedents and plural pronouns with plural antecedents. Be careful not to mix singular and plural forms. Sentence A is not correct because "group" is singular, while "their" is plural. Similarly, sentence C is not correct because "student" is singular, while "their" is plural. Sentence D is not correct because "friends" is plural, while "he or she" is singular.

24) The correct answer is D. There will be some questions on the exam that test your knowledge of verb forms and usage. In this sentence, you are stating a general principle, so the present simple form "are" needs to be used.

25) The correct answer is D. Sentence D is incorrect because the reader cannot be sure whether the phrase "warmth all year round" applies to Florida or to another state that has not been mentioned. The other sentences correctly position the adjectival phrase "warm all year round" immediately before the noun "Florida."

26) The correct answer is D. For questions on clear pronouns, look at each sentence to see if there is any doubt about what the pronoun refers to. In sentence A, we do not know if "he" refers

to Terry or his brother. In sentence B, we have no way of knowing who "they" are. In sentence C, we do not know if Washington itself is beautiful or if the cherry blossoms are beautiful.

27) The correct answer is C. Sentence C is incorrect because it lacks the word "so" before the word "is." It also needs a comma after the word "way."

28) The correct answer is B. Remember that reference to research will have more authority than other sources. However, also bear in mind that your reference must be relevant to your topic. If you are discussing only children, you would not want evidence to support large families. Therefore, answer B provides the least support.

29) The correct answer is C. This is another question on parallelism. Answer C is correct because "cookies" and "cake" are both nouns. The other sentences mix different forms.

30) The correct answer is A. This is another question on pronoun-antecedent agreement. "Friends" is plural, so the pronoun "their" is needed. Do not confuse "their" with the contraction "they're" or with the location word "there."

PERT READING PRACTICE TEST 2

Read the selections and answer the questions that follow.

The Mechanics of Motion

The question of the mechanics of motion is complex and one that has a protracted history. Much has been discovered about gravity, defined as the force that draws objects to the earth, both before and since the British mathematician Sir Isaac Newton mused upon the subject in the 17th century. As early as the third century BC, a Greek philosopher and natural scientist named Aristotle conducted a great deal of scientific investigation into the subject. Most of Aristotle's life was devoted to the study of the objects of natural science, and it is for this work that he is most renowned. The Greek scientist wrote a tome entitled *Metaphysics*, which contains the observations that he made as a result of performing this original research in the natural sciences.

Several centuries later, in the first century AD, Ptolemy, another Greek scientist, was credited with a nascent, yet unformulated theory, that there was a force that moved toward the center of the earth, thereby holding objects on its surface. Although later ridiculed for his belief that the earth was the center of the planetary system, Aristotle's compatriot nevertheless did contribute to the development of the theory of gravity.

It was during the period called the renaissance that gravitational forces were perhaps studied most widely. An astronomer, Galileo Galilei corrected one of Aristotle's erring theories by pointing out that objects of differing weights fall to earth at the same speed. Years later, Descartes, who was known at that time as a dilettante philosopher, but was later dubbed the father of modern mathematics, held that a body in circular motion constantly strives to recede from the center. This theory added weight to the notion that bodies in motion had their own forces.

Newton took these studies a step further and used them to show that the earth's rotation does not fling bodies into the air because the force of gravity, measured by the rate of falling bodies, is greater than the centrifugal force arising from the rotation. In his first mathematical formulation of gravity, published in 1687, Newton posited that the same force that kept the moon from being propelled away from the earth also applied to gravity at the earth's surface. While this finding, termed the Law of Universal Gravitation, is said to have been occasioned by Newton's observation of the fall of an apple from a tree in the orchard at his home, in reality, the idea did not come to the scientist in a flash of inspiration, but was developed slowly over time.

Newton had the prescience to appreciate that his study was of great import for the scientific community and for society as a whole. It is because of Newton's work that we currently understand the effect of gravity on the earth as a global system. For instance, as a result of Newton's investigation into the subject of gravity, we know that geological features such as mountains and canyons can cause variances in the Earth's gravitational force. Newton is also to be acknowledged for the realization that the force of gravity becomes less robust as the distance from the equator diminishes, due to the rotation of the earth, as well as the declining mass and density of the planet from the equator to the poles.

1) The best definition of the word "prescience" as it is used in the selection is:

   A. pre-scientific

   B. hindsight

   C. investigation

   D. perception

2) According to the selection, what conclusion can be drawn about Aristotle?

   A. He was the founder of the Law of Universal Gravitation.

   B. He was best known for producing error-free work.

   C. He was a famous Greek natural scientist.

   D. He was a contemporary of Ptolemy.

3) Which of the following statements best expresses the main idea of the selection?

   A. The study of the mechanics of motion has developed over many centuries.

   B. The study of the mechanics of motion would not have been initiated without the work of Ptolemy and Aristotle.

C. The law of gravity is directly related to the study of the mechanics of motion.

D. Newton's study of gravitational forces has proven to be of invaluable significance to us today.

How to Bake a Cake

Baking a cake is easy, provided you have a good oven and the correct ingredients. For a moist and fluffy cake, you should first of all pre-heat the oven to 350 degrees Fahrenheit. Be absolutely sure that the oven is pre-heated to the correct temperature. While the oven is pre-heating, you can grease and flour your cake pan and mix your ingredients together.

Before adding the wet ingredients, mix the dry ingredients together. The latter consists of one and a half cups of sugar, one teaspoon of salt, two teaspoons of baking soda, and two cups of sifted flour, which should be mixed well in a large bowl. However, before proceeding with the mixture, ensure that the bowl is of a sufficient size to accommodate all of the ingredients. Now add one-half cup of vegetable shortening, two eggs, one cup of whole milk, and a teaspoon of vanilla.

Put the mixture into the cake pan, bake for 30 minutes, and enjoy!

4) Based on the instructions above, it is likely that failing to pre-heat the oven will result in:

    A. the cake being burned.

    B. the cake taking longer to bake.

    C. insufficient time to prepare the cake pan.

    D. the cake being dry and dense.

5) What should one do after preparing the cake pan?

    A. add the wet ingredients

    B. check that the mixing bowl is large enough

    C. mix the sugar, salt, baking soda, and flour together

    D. add the shortening, eggs, milk, and vanilla

The Antarctic Ice Sheet

Containing nearly seventy percent of the world's freshwater supply, Antarctica plays a crucial role in the world's ecosphere. The corpus of research on Antarctica has resulted in an abundance of factual data. For example, we now know that more than ninety-nine percent of the land is completely covered by snow and ice, making Antarctica the coldest and iciest continent on the planet.

This inhospitable climate has brought about the adaptation of a plethora of plants and biological organisms present on the continent. An investigation into the sedimentary geological formations provides testimony to the process of adaptation. Ancient sediments recovered from the bottom of Antarctic lakes, bacteria as well as discovered in the ice itself, has revealed the history of changes to the ice sheet over the past 10,000 years.

The Antarctic is a key factor in current global climate change. On its surface, the continent possesses a four kilometer thick ice sheet. This mammoth sheet of ice atrophies because of year-round melting at its base, as well as the loss of ice due to the formation of icebergs. However, the ice sheet is also perpetually replenished by snowfall and frost.

At present, two methodologies are employed to measure the size of the ice sheet. The first is the accumulation method, by which the difference between the loss of ice and the accumulation of new precipitation is calculated. The second technique, known as the direct measurement approach, involves the use of satellites to determine whether the ice sheet is growing thicker or thinner. Unfortunately, both methods have a rather large potential for error.

The measurement of the ice sheet is of paramount importance because scientists fear that the melting of a large amount of the ice sheet may occur as a result of global warming. Some believe that human beings are directly responsible for any potential ecological catastrophe, pointing to our excessive reliance on fossil fuels for domestic use and transportation. On the other hand, others assert that natural causes also have a part to play in the debacle, especially volcanic eruptions. While there are some uncertainties about the phenomenon of global warming, it is indisputable that the current rate of sea level change is unprecedented.

The melting of the ice sheet inevitably leads to a dramatic rise in sea levels. Recent research suggests that climate change has already caused the oceans to raise ten to twenty centimeters. Computer models are currently being used to predict the probability of further sea level increases, but many scientists fear that even with a small sea level rise, nations and cultures that have existed for millennia may be destroyed.

6) According to the selection, the plants and organisms in Antarctica:

    A. have survived because of the process of adaptation.

    B. are the result of sedimentary geological formations.

    C. cover more than 99% of the land surface.

    D. reveal the history of changes to the ice sheet over the past 10,000 years.

7) Which of the following would provide the best support for the assertion that Antarctica plays a crucial role in the world's ecosphere?

    A. a direct quotation from one of the key researchers on climate change

    B. a comparison of Antarctica's ecosphere to the ecosphere of another continent

    C. a measurement of the precise dimensions of the ice sheet covering Antarctica

    D. empirical evidence from a specific study that has investigated changes to the Antarctic ice sheet

Don't Worry – Be Happy

Almost everyone has heard the hit single "Don't Worry, Be Happy" by Bobby McFerrin. The song has a very repetitive way of conveying its message. McFerrin's refrain was that everyone can feel happy by simply choosing not to worry.

Living a happy and worry-free life is a wonderful ideal, but it must be said that life is full of stresses and strains that are often not of our own choosing. One of the truest things ever said is that the only thing in life that will always remain the same is change.

In addition to causing us to worry, stress is linked to the top causes of death, such as heart disease, cancer, and stroke. So, achieving happiness in today's society is often a complex, multi-dimensional process.

Choose to Be Happy

Abraham Lincoln observed that happiness is a choice for most people. This echoes the claims of the Dalai Lama, who stated that people can decide whether they will be happy or not through self-discipline. So, isn't the choice simple really? Shouldn't we choose to be happy?

Being happy occurs when we choose not to worry. This choice is based on a thankful attitude. We have so much to be thankful for. Thank the taxi driver for bringing you home safely, thank the cook for a wonderful dinner, and thank the person who cleans your windows. When we give thanks to others whenever possible, we choose the path of gratitude that leads to the road to happiness.

8) With which of the following ideas do both selections agree?

   A. Happiness is the result of decisions we make.

   B. Most people are not thankful enough.

   C. Many people lack of self-discipline.

   D. Worry has a direct impact on happiness.

9) How would the writer of selection 2 most likely respond to the following statement from selection 1?: "It must be said that life is full of stresses and strains that are often not of our own choosing."

   A. People who experience stress are ungrateful for the positive aspects of their lives.

   B. Abraham Lincoln and the Dalai Lama also experienced stress.

   C. It may be true that we cannot choose certain events in life, but we can still choose to be happy.

   D. Stressed-out people lack self-discipline generally.

The Theories of Jean Piaget

Born in France in 1896, Jean Piaget went on to become one of the most influential thinkers in the areas of educational psychology and child development in the twentieth and twenty-first centuries. The primary thrust of his research revolved around the question: "How do human beings come to know?" His research culminated in the groundbreaking discovery of what he called "abstract symbolic reasoning." The basic idea behind this principle was that biology influences child development to a greater extent than does socialization. That is to say, Piaget concluded that younger children answered research questions differently than older ones not because they were less intelligent, but because their intelligence was at a lower stage of biological development.

Because he was a biologist, Piaget had a keen interest in the adaptation of organisms to their environment, and this preoccupation led to many astute observations. Piaget found that behavior in children was controlled by mental organizations called "schemes," which enable an individual to interpret his or her world and respond to situations. Piaget coined the term "equilibration" to describe the biological need of human beings to balance these schemes against the processes of environmental adaptation.

The French-born biologist postulated that schemes are innate since all children are born with these drives. Noting that while other animals continued to deploy their in-born schemes throughout the entire duration of their lives, Piaget hypothesized that human beings' pre-existing, innate schemes compete with and ultimately diverge from constructed schemes, which are socially-acquired in the environmental adaptation process.

As Piaget's research with children progressed, he identified four stages of cognitive development. In the first stage, which he termed the sensorimotor stage, Piaget noted that at the incipience of the child's mental development, intelligence is displayed by way of the infant's physical interactions with the world. That is, the child's intelligence is directly correlated to his or her mobility and motor activity. Children begin to develop some language skills, as well as memory, which Piaget called "object permanence," during this initial stage.

When the child becomes a toddler, he or she enters the pre-operational stage. During this stage the child is largely egocentric, meaning that intellectual and emotional energy is directed inwardly, rather than on other individuals. Although memory, language, and intelligence continue to develop during these years, thinking is illogical and inflexible on the whole.

Next, the child begins the concrete operational stage. Beginning roughly at age five, this stage is characterized by the appearance of logical and systematic thought processes. In this stage, the child begins to conceptualize symbols and measurements relating to concrete objects, such as numbers, weights, lengths, and volumes. As the child's intelligence becomes more logical, egocentrism begins to dissipate.

At the commencement of the teenage years, the final stage, called the formal operational stage, is initiated. During this stage, the individual should be able to grasp abstract thought on a range of complex ideas and theories. Unfortunately, recent research has shown that adults in many countries around the globe have failed to complete Piaget's formal operational phase stage, perhaps owing to poverty or poor educational opportunities.

10) Which of the following best supports the author's assertion that Piaget continues to be one of the most influential thinkers in the areas of educational psychology and child development in the twenty-first century?

    A.   the explanation that Piaget's background was in the study of biology

    B.   the fact that Piaget coined many terms to describe biological needs

    C.   the mention of poor educational opportunities around the globe

    D.   the reference to the use of Piaget's theories in recent research

11) According to the selection, which of the following statements best characterizes the sensorimotor stage?

    A.   The growth of the child's intelligence in this stage depends predominantly on his or her verbal ability.

    B.   The skills obtained during this stage are of less importance than those achieved during later developmental stages.

    C.   During this stage, the child learns how his or her mobility relates to language.

D. The child's cognitive development in this stage is achieved through physical movement in his or her environment.

12) According to the selection, the reader can conclude that the formal operational stage:

A. is the result of poor economic conditions.

B. has not yet been finished by many individuals around the world.

C. is an important global problem.

D. is based on complicated scientific theories.

Stone Age Artists

(1) In Southern Spain and France, Stone Age artists painted stunning drawings on the walls of caves nearly 30,000 years ago. (2) Painting pictures of the animals upon which they relied for food, the artists worked by the faint light of lamps that were made of animal fat and twigs.

(3) In addition to having to work in relative darkness, the artists had to endure great physical discomfort since the inner chambers of the caves were sometimes less than one meter in height. (4) Thus, the artists had to crouch or squat uncomfortably as they practiced their craft.

(5) Their paints were mixed from natural elements such as yellow ochre, clay, calcium carbonate, and iron oxide. (6) However, many other natural elements and minerals were not used. (7) An analysis of the cave paintings reveals that the colors of the paints used by the artists ranged from light yellow to dark black.

(8) The artists utilized ochre and manganese as engraving tools in order first to etch their outlines on the walls of the caves. (9) Before removing their lamps and leaving their creations to dry, they painted the walls with brushes of animal hair or feathers. (10) Archeologists have also discovered that ladders and scaffolding were used in higher areas of the caves.

13) Which of the following best describes the author's purpose in the selection?

A. To show surprise that the tools of Stone Age artists were similar to those that artists use today.

B. To express admiration of both the Stone Age artists' craft and their ability to paint such beautiful creations, in spite of the extreme conditions they faced.

C. To lament the poor esthetic quality of the paintings.

D. To imply that it is predictable and banal that Stone Age artists would paint pictures of animals.

14) Which sentence is least relevant to the main idea of the selection?

A. Sentence 4

B. Sentence 5

C. Sentence 6

D. Sentence 7

Bad Service in the Service Industry

Diners in restaurants sometimes ask why their servers aren't able to cope with some of their requests. Is it fair to suggest that members of the service industry typically deliver below-par service to customers? Consider a simple example of a fast food restaurant. Chances are that you've been at the receiving end of some bad service at some point in time. Is it then fair to assume that staff who wear work uniforms are simply to be tagged with a warning sign that they will not deliver to their clientele?

To fully understand the reasons for occasional bad service, the factors influencing the situation need to be considered. Perhaps the person providing the service was new to his or her job. Maybe he or she was a trainee and was not able to perform without the assistance of a supervisor. In addition, service people can experience a great deal of stress when trying to do several things at once for different patrons.

Factors Influencing Service Quality

Whether in the fast food service or in a legal firm, there are countless factors that can influence the outcome of the service provided. However, the fact remains that a person who wears a suit to work is less likely to make a mistake than someone in the service industry.

The hurried pace and pressure to perform in the service industry cause mistakes to occur. Those who do office work have the luxury of working in less stressful environments. They have more time to check their work for mistakes before delivering it to their clients.

15) The writer of selection 1 would probably take the most offense with which one of the following claims from selection 2?

    A. Whether in the fast food service or in a legal firm, there are countless factors that can influence the outcome of the service provided.

    B. A person who wears a suit to work is less likely to make a mistake than someone in the service industry.

    C. The hurried pace and pressure to perform in the service industry cause mistakes to occur.

    D. Those who do office work have the luxury of working in less stressful environments.

16) The writers of both selections would agree that:

    A. office workers are less likely to make mistakes than service people.

    B. lawyers work more conscientiously than wait staff.

    C. the clothes a person wears can affect work performance.

    D. the service industry can be extremely stressful at times.

The Study of Philosophy

The study of philosophy usually deals with two key problem areas: human choice and human thought. A consideration of these problem areas is not an aspect of psychology or art. The first problem area, human choice, asks whether human beings can really make decisions that will change their futures. Conversely, it also investigates to what extent the individual's future is fixed and pre-determined by cosmic forces outside the control of human beings. In the second problem area, human thought, epistemology is considered. "Epistemology" means the study of knowledge; it should not be confused with ontology, the study of being or existence.

17) In the selection, the reference to "psychology or art" provides:

    A.   an inappropriate example.

    B.   irrelevant information.

    C.   an obscure shift in focus.

    D.   a comparison to other academic disciplines.

Abraham Lincoln

(1) In the fall of 1859, a discouraged man was sitting in his run-down law office in Springfield, Illinois. (2) He was fifty years old, in debt, and had been a lawyer for twenty years, earning on average 3,000 dollars a year. (3) This man would later go on to do great things for his country. (4) His name was Abraham Lincoln.

(5) In spite of these obvious financial constraints, some of Abraham Lincoln's associates had already begun to put forward the idea that he should run for president of the United States, a notion that Mr. Lincoln discounted in his usual self-deprecating manner. (6) Yet, in 1858, Lincoln began to write influential Republican Party leaders for their assistance. (7) By 1860, Lincoln had garnered more public support, after having delivered public lectures and political speeches in various states. (8) Although he was the underdog, Lincoln won 354 of the 466 total nominations at the Republican National Convention and was later elected as President of the United States.

18) In the selection, sentence 6:

    A.   refutes the veracity of the facts provided in sentence 5.

    B.   provides a contrast to the background information provided in sentence 5.

    C.   uses an example to introduce unexpected information in sentence 7.

    D.   paraphrases the ideas given in sentence 7.

The Electron Microscope

(1) An efficient electron microscope can magnify an object by more than one million times its original size. (2) This innovation has thereby allowed scientists to study the precise molecules that constitute human life.

(3) The electron microscope functions by emitting a stream of electrons from a gun-type instrument, which is similar to the apparatus used in a television tube. (4) The electrons pass through an advanced electronic field that is accelerated to millions of volts in certain cases. (5) Before traveling through a vacuum in order to remove oxygen molecules, the electrons are focused into a beam by way of magnetic coils.

(6) Invisible to the naked eye, electron beams can nevertheless be projected onto a florescent screen. (7) When striking the screen, the electrons glow and can even be recorded on film. (8) Cameras can also use film to capture images.

(9) In the transmission electron microscope, which is used to study cells or tissues, the beam passes through a thin slice of the specimen that is being studied. (10) On the other hand, in the scanning electron microscope, which is used for tasks such as examining bullets and fibers, the beam is reflected. (11) This reflection creates a picture of the specimen line by line.

19) Sentence 10 provides the reader with:

    A.   relevant examples of modern-day applications for electron microscopes.

    B.   an explanation of the differences in functionality of the two different types of electron microscopes.

    C.   a contrast between old and new microscope technologies.

    D.   a clarification of the manner in which electron beams are formed.

Excerpt from *A Story of the Days to Come*

The excellent Mr. Morris was an Englishman, and he lived in the days of Queen Victoria the Good. He was a prosperous and very sensible man; he read the *Times* and went to church, and as he grew towards middle age, so too did an expression of quiet contented contempt for all who were not as himself settled. Everything that it was right and proper for a man in his position to possess, he possessed.

And among other right and proper possessions, this Mr. Morris had a wife and children. They were the right sort of wife, and the right sort and number of children, of course; nothing imaginative or highty-flighty about any of them, so far as Mr. Morris could see; they wore perfectly correct clothing, neither silly nor faddy in any way; and they lived in a nice sensible house.

And when it was a fit and proper thing for him to do so, Mr. Morris died. His tomb was of marble, and, without any art nonsense or laudatory inscription, quietly imposing—such being the fashion of his time.

20) What is the best meaning of "highty-flighty" as it is used in the selection?

    A. empty-headed

    B. erudite

    C. sensitive

    D. unfriendly

21) The description of Mr. Morris's home and his tomb are similar because:

    A. they demonstrated no real interest in the future of mankind.

    B. they displayed the underlying resentment that Mr. Morris felt about his life.

    C. they would have been considered right and proper for the society of their time.

    D. they both reveal the heed and care that society takes about the future.

Excerpt from "Adoption of the Declaration of Human Rights"

Delivered by Eleanor Roosevelt, 1948

We stand today at the threshold of a great event both in the life of the United Nations and in the life of mankind, that is the approval by the General Assembly of the Declaration of Human Rights. This declaration may well become the international Magna Carta of all people everywhere. We hope its proclamation by the General Assembly will be an event comparable to the proclamation of the Declaration of the Rights of Man by the French people in 1789, the adoption of the Bill of Rights by the people of the United States, and the adoption of comparable declarations at different times in other countries.

22) Within the selection, the references to the Magna Carta, the Declaration of the Rights of Man, and the Bill of Rights are used to support the speaker's intention to:

    A.   incite dissent among the audience members.

    B.   emphasize the historical importance of this event.

    C.   persuade her opponents to support this declaration.

    D.   perpetuate the status quo.

23) Which of the following search terms would be best to type into a search engine in the Internet in order to find the complete version of this speech?

    A.   Eleanor Roosevelt, 1948

    B.   Speeches delivered about human rights

    C.   Public speeches 1948

    D.   Adoption of the Declaration of Human Rights

The History of Polyphonic Music

(1) Polyphonic music appeared in the fifteen century during the early Renaissance period. (2) As polyphony developed, musical traditions began to change, and this meant that music began to rely on a greater range of voices.

(3) During the sixteenth century, there was an attempt to return to the tradition of Greek drama. (4) This had an extremely positive impact on the opera. (5) As a result, the opera expanded to include oratorios, which are sung musical compositions on a particular subject. (6) This phenomenon occurred in the Italian opera, and so, the opera, in turn, influenced the musical style of the early seventeenth century.

(7) The seventeenth century also witnessed the proliferation of musical instruments. (8) Musical compositions and arrangements for keyboard instruments, such as the piano and organ, thrived during this period.

(9) The eighteenth century was marked by the development of baroque music. (10) This century was dominated by two German-born geniuses: Bach and Handel. (11) These two composers wrote music in almost every genre, including opera and oratorio music.

(12) Beethoven is the crucial link between the classical and romantic periods. (13) To his compositions, he added deeper texture, meaning the depth and breadth of different types of musical sound. (14) For this reason, the music of Beethoven is commonly regarded as establishing the end of the classical period.

24) Which of the following sentences uses language that is unbiased?

    A. Sentence 4

    B. Sentence 6

    C. Sentence 10

    D. Sentence 12

Fast Food

Most people would rather eat fast food than prepare a meal at home.

Many local residents complain about the lack of fast food restaurants in the city.

25) What does the second sentence do?

    A.   It presents a solution to the problem mentioned in the first sentence.

    B.   It gives unexpected information.

    C.   It reinforces the claim made in first sentence.

    D.   It provides an example for what is stated in the first sentence.

What Causes Cancer?

Cancer occurs when cells in the body begin to divide abnormally and form more cells without control or order. There are some factors which are known to increase the risk of cancer.

Smoking is the largest single cause of death from cancer in the United States. One-third of the deaths from cancer each year are related to smoking, making tobacco use the most preventable cause of death in this country.

In addition, poor food choices increase cancer risk. Research shows that there is a definite link between the consumption of high-fat food and cancer.

If a cell divides when it is not necessary, a large growth called a tumor can form. These tumors can usually be removed, and in many cases, they do not come back. However, in some cases the cancer from the original tumor spreads. The spread of cancer in this way is called metastasis.

26) From the selection, it can be inferred that:

    A.   a low-fat diet can reduce the risk of cancer.

    B.   the consumption of high-fat food has increased in recent years.

    C.   most cancer sufferers have made poor food choices.

    D.   smoking always causes cells to divide abnormally.

Excerpt from *Oliver Twist*

Oliver, having taken down the shutters, was graciously assisted by Noah, who having consoled him with the assurance that "he'd catch it," condescended to help him. Mr. Snowberry came down soon after.

Shortly afterwards, Mrs. Snowberry appeared. Oliver having "caught it," in fulfillment of Noah's prediction, followed the young gentleman down the stairs to breakfast.

"Come near the fire, Noah," said Charlotte. "I have saved a nice little bit of bacon for you from master's breakfast."

"Do you hear?" said Noah.

"Lord, Noah!" said Charlotte.

"Let him alone!" said Noah. "Why everybody lets him alone enough, for the matter of that."

"Oh, you strange soul!" said Charlotte, bursting into a hearty laugh. She was then joined by Noah, after which they both looked scornfully at poor Oliver Twist.

Noah was a charity boy, but not a workhouse orphan. He could trace his genealogy back to his parents, who lived hard by; his mother being a washerwoman, and his father a drunken soldier, discharged with a wooden leg, and a diurnal pension of twopence-halfpenny and an unstable fraction. The shop boys in the neighborhood had long been in the habit of branding Noah, in the public streets, with the ignominious epithets of "leathers," "charity," and the like; and Noah had borne them without reply. But now that fortune had cast his way a nameless orphan, at whom even the meanest could point the finger of scorn, he retorted on him with interest.

27) The selection mainly illustrates:

    A. Charlotte's contempt of orphans.

    B. the wealth of the Snowberry family.

    C. the adventures and exploits of Oliver.

    D. the relationship between Noah and Oliver.

The HSBC Skyscraper

(1) The Hong Kong and Shanghai Bank Corporation (HSBC) skyscraper in Hong Kong is one of the world's most famous high-rise buildings. (2) The building was designed so that it had many pre-built parts that were not constructed on site. (3) This prefabrication made the project a truly international effort. (4) The windows were manufactured in Austria, the exterior walls were fabricated in the United States, the toilets and air-conditioning were made in Japan, and many of the other components came from Germany.

(5) The HSBC tower consists of 47 stories, which is an immense contrast to the twenty-story buildings in its vicinity. (6) The construction of other buildings nearby was impeded by the soft, water-logged ground in the area. (7) For this reason, the ground water supply had to be carefully assessed prior to construction of the HSBC building. (8) This assessment was necessary in order to ensure that subsidence, and potentially collapse of the new structure, could be averted.

28) Which of the following words does NOT describe the tone of sentence 6?

   A. informative

   B. succinct

   C. significant

   D. loquacious

The Input Hypothesis

According to Stephen Krashen's input hypothesis, a language learner improves his or her language skills when he or she is exposed to language input such as lectures or reading materials that are one level above the learner's current level of language ability. Language output such as verbal or written expressions are not seen to have any direct effect of the learner's ability.

29) The selection suggests that the input hypothesis is:

   A. a theory that assumes that all language learners begin at the same level of ability.

B. a theory that asserts that learners can best improve their language skills when their learning is appropriately challenging.

C. a school of thought that discounts the importance of traditional grammatical skills.

D. a system of language rules established by Stephen Krashen that learners of new languages try to follow.

Measuring Brain Activity

Our ability to measure brain activity is owing to the research of two European scientists. It was in 1929 that electrical activity in the human brain was first discovered. Hans Berger, the German psychiatrist who made the discovery, was despondent to find out, however, that many other scientists quickly dismissed his research. The work of Berger was confirmed three years later when Edgar Adrian, a Briton, clearly demonstrated that the brain, like the heart, is profuse in its electrical activity. Because of Adrian's work, we know that the electrical impulses in the brain are a mixture of four different frequencies. By "frequency," we are referring to the number of electrical impulses that occur in the brain per second. These four frequencies are called alpha, beta, delta, and theta.

In order to measure brain activity and function, various types of equipment can perform various types of tests. We have traditionally used CAT and PET scans for this purpose. The PET scan (which works by means of an inert radioactive substance given to a patient) allows the doctor to observe the movement of the substance through the brain. On the other hand, the CAT scan is like an X-ray of the brain, which is displayed on a computer screen.

The PET scan shows up as one image and that image will have different colors. Each one of the colors displays the pattern of the brain activity. The CAT scan is displayed as a cross-section (unlike the PET scan), so it can be viewed from different angles or positions. As far as patients are concerned, the CAT is far less invasive because they don't need to ingest a radioactive substance beforehand.

In addition to CAT and PET scans, we have the MRI scan, which works according to the principles of magnetism. The MRI is perhaps the most indispensable of all of the various scans due to its ability to map the brain in three dimensions.

30) Which of the following details best contributes to the credibility of the information contained in the selection?

    A. the parenthetical details

    B. the names of two European scientists

    C. the mention of the four frequencies of brain waves

    D. the advanced grammar and sentence structures

PERT READING PRACTICE TEST 2 – ANSWERS AND EXPLANATIONS

1) The correct answer is D. For questions like this one, remember to look for synonyms in the same paragraph as the unknown word. The sentence tells us that Newton's work was of great import. The paragraph goes on to say that Newton helped us understand the laws of gravity. The word "understanding" is a synonym for "perception", so answer D is the best choice.

2) The correct answer is C. The first paragraph tells us that Aristotle was a "Greek philosopher and natural scientist."

3) The correct answer is A. The main idea of the selection is that the study of the mechanics of motion has developed over many centuries. The selection gives a chronological account of the study of the mechanics of motion, beginning with the third century BC in paragraph 1 and ending with current research in the last paragraph.

4) The correct answer is D. Failing to pre-heat the oven will result in the cake being dry and dense. Paragraph 1 of the selection states: "For a moist and fluffy cake, you should first of all pre-heat the oven to 350 degrees Fahrenheit." The opposite of moist is dry, and the opposite of fluffy is dense.

5) The correct answer is B. Be careful with questions like this because the sentences in the selection may not be given in the correct order. Notice the sentence: "However, before proceeding with the mixture, ensure that the bowl is of a sufficient size." This indicates that you must check the size of the bowl after preparing the pan and before mixing the ingredients.

6) The correct answer is A. According to the selection, the plants and organisms in Antarctica have survived because of the process of adaptation. This answer is supported by the first sentence of the second paragraph, which states: "This inhospitable climate has brought about the adaptation of a plethora of plants and biological organisms present on the continent."

7) The correct answer A. Reference to a specific researcher by name will have more credibility and authority than reference to research studies in general. However, the reference provided must also be directly relevant to the theme of the selection. In this selection, our main theme is the Antarctic ice sheet, not climate change. For this reason, answer A is not the best answer, even though it refers to a key researcher. Therefore, reference to a specific study on the ice sheet would provide the best support for the assertions in the selection.

8) The correct answer is D. The writer of selection 1 discusses the impact of worry on life events. The writer of selection 2 states that "being happy occurs when we choose not to worry." So, both writers would agree that worry has a direct impact on happiness.

9) The correct answer is C. The writer of selection 2 emphasizes that personal choice is the most significant factor in being happy, so he would disagree with the idea that unhappiness can be caused by events outside of the control of human choice.

10) The correct answer is D. The reference to the use of Piaget's theories in recent research in the last paragraph of the selection best supports the assertion that Piaget continues to be influential in the twenty-first century because it relates Piaget's work to the present day.

11) The correct answer is D. Paragraph 4 states that in the sensorimotor stage "the child's . . . intelligence is displayed by way of the infant's physical interactions with the world." In other words, the child's cognitive development in this stage is achieved through physical movement in his or her environment.

12) The correct answer is B. The final paragraph states that "adults in many countries around the globe have failed to complete Piaget's formal operational phase stage, perhaps owing to poverty or poor educational opportunities."

13) The correct answer is B. The purpose of the writer is to express amazement that Stone Age artists were able to paint such beautiful creations in spite of the extreme conditions they faced. For questions like this one, look for adjectives in the passage that give hints about the author's point of view. The phrase "stunning drawings" in paragraph one indicates the author's admiration of the artists and their craft.

14) The correct answer is C. Sentence 6 states: "However, many other natural elements and minerals were not used." The selection is analyzing the paints that the artists used, as well as their artistic technique and working conditions, so mentioning something which was not used in their process is least relevant to the main idea of the selection.

15) The correct answer is B. The writer of selection 1 poses the following rhetorical question: "Is it then fair to assume that staff who wear work uniforms are simply to be tagged with a warning sign that they will not deliver to their clientele?" She then goes on to refute this idea in the remainder of selection 1. Accordingly, the writer of selection 1 would disagree with the assertion

from selection 2 that "a person who wears a suit to work is less likely to make a mistake than someone in the service industry."

16) The correct answer is D. The writer of selection 1 mentions that "service people can experience a great deal of stress when trying to do several things at once for different patrons." The writer of selection 2 talks about "the hurried pace and pressure to perform in the service industry." So, both writers would agree that service industry can be extremely stressful at times.

17) The correct answer is B. In the selection, the reference to "psychology or art" provides irrelevant information because the selection focuses on philosophy, not psychology or art. You may be tempted to choose answer C, but the focus has not been shifted because only one sentence provides the irrelevant information. In other words, there is no shift in focus because the remainder of the selection goes on to talk about philosophy, which is the main theme of the selection.

18) The correct answer is B. Sentence 6 provides a contrast to the background information provided in sentence 5. We can see that a contrast is being set up in sentence 6 because it begins with the word "yet." In addition, sentence 5 asserts that Lincoln discounted (or disagreed with) the idea that he should run for President, while sentence 6 shows that Lincoln had started his Presidential campaign by writing influential Republican Party leaders for their assistance.

19) The correct answer is B. Sentence 10 provides the reader with an explanation of the differences in functionality of the two different types of electron microscopes. The phrase "on the other hand" at the beginning of sentence 10 indicates that differences are going to be mentioned. Moreover, the answer is also clear from the content of the sentences. Sentence 9 discusses the transmission electron microscope, while sentence 10 describes the scanning electron microscope.

20) The correct answer is A. Paragraph 2 describes how Mr. Morris had "the right sort and number of children." So, the reader can assume that Mr. Morris's children, like Mr. Morris himself, conform to social convention by trying to be responsible and logical. In other words, his children were not empty-headed or "highty-flighty."

21) The correct answer is C. The narrator tells us that Mr. Morris's home was "a nice sensible house," and his tomb is described as "being the fashion of his time." The reader can therefore

deduce that both the house and the tomb would have been considered right and proper for the society of their time.

22) The correct answer is B. The references to the Magna Carta, the Declaration of the Rights of Man, and the Bill of Rights are used to support the speaker's intention to emphasize the historical importance of this event. The historical importance of the event is also highlighted in the speech, when the speaker asserts: "We stand today at the threshold of a great event."

23) The correct answer is D. In order to find a complete version of a speech online, you would need to type in the title of the speech. The title of the speech is provided before the speaker's name at the top of the selection. Looking at this selection, we can see that the title of the speech is: "Adoption of the Declaration of Human Rights."

24) The correct answer is B. Sentence 6 uses neutral, unbiased language. Sentence 4 expresses bias in the words "extremely positive." Sentence 10 expresses bias in the word "geniuses" and sentence 12 in the word "crucial."

25) The correct answer is C. The claim about people's preferences for fast food, which is made in first sentence, is reinforced in the second sentence by the complaints about the lack of fast food restaurants in the city. Note that the second sentence is not an example, since examples of specific food preferences are not provided.

26) The correct answer is A. The inference that a low-fat diet can reduce the risk of cancer can be drawn from this selection. The reverse of this idea is provided in the last sentence of the third paragraph, which states that "research shows that there is a definite link between the consumption of high-fat food and cancer."

27) The correct answer is D. The selection mainly illustrates the relationship between Noah and Oliver. This idea is illustrated especially clearly in the last paragraph of the selection, in which we see Noah's view of Oliver.

28) The correct answer is D. "Loquacious" means verbose or wordy. Sentence 6 is informative and to the point, so it cannot be described as loquacious.

29) The correct answer is B. The selection suggests that learners best improve their language skills when their learning is appropriately challenging. The selection states that "a language learner improves his or her language skills when he or she is exposed to language input such

as lectures or reading materials that are one level above the learner's current level of language ability." The phrase "one level above the learner's current level" indicates that their learning is appropriately challenging.

30) The correct answer is B. The names of two European scientists, Hans Berger and Edgar Adrian, best contribute to the credibility of the information contained in the selection. As stated previously, quotations from or references to specific researchers generally lend the most credibility or authority to a selection.

PERT WRITING PRACTICE TEST 2

1) Choose the word or words that best complete the sentence.

   The child tried to grab the cookies from the shelf, but _____ out of reach.

   A. was

   B. it was

   C. they were

   D. he is

2) Which of the following sentences is written correctly?

   A. Covered in chocolate frosting, the hostess dropped the cake in front of all the guests.

   B. The cake fell from the table onto the floor in front of all the guests, which was covered in chocolate frosting.

   C. Covered in chocolate frosting, the cake fell from the table onto the floor in front of all the guests.

   D. Covered in chocolate frosting, the guests saw the hostess drop the cake.

3) Which of the following sentences uses correct parallel structure?

   A. To love and be loved is the greatest happiness of existence.

   B. Loving and be loved is the greatest happiness of existence.

   C. Loving and to be loved is the greatest happiness of existence.

   D. To love and being loved is the greatest happiness of existence.

Read the selection and answer the question.

The Electron Microscope

(1) An efficient electron microscope can magnify an object by more than one million times its original size. (2) This innovation has thereby allowed scientists to study the precise molecules that constitute human life.

(3) The electron microscope functions by emitting a stream of electrons from a gun-type instrument, which is similar to the apparatus used in a television tube. (4) The electrons pass through an advanced electronic field that is accelerated to millions of volts in certain cases. (5) Before traveling through a vacuum in order to remove oxygen molecules, the electrons are focused into a beam by way of magnetic coils.

(6) Invisible to the naked eye, electron beams can nevertheless be projected onto a florescent screen. (7) When striking the screen, the electrons glow and can even be recorded on film. (8) Cameras can also use film to capture images.

(9) In the transmission electron microscope, which is used to study cells or tissues, the beam passes through a thin slice of the specimen that is being studied. (10) On the other hand, in the scanning electron microscope, which is used for tasks such as examining bullets and fibers, the beam is reflected. (11) This reflection creates a picture of the specimen line by line.

4) Which sentence does not belong in the selection?

    A.   Sentence 2

    B.   Sentence 3

    C.   Sentence 8

    D.   Sentence 11

Read the selection and answer the questions.

The HSBC Skyscraper

(1) The Hong Kong and Shanghai Bank Corporation (HSBC) skyscraper in Hong Kong is one of the world's most famous high-rise buildings. (2) The building was designed so that it had many pre-built parts that were not constructed on site. (3) This prefabrication made the project a truly international effort. (4) The windows were manufactured in Austria, the exterior walls were fabricated in the United States, the toilets and air-conditioning were made in Japan, and many of the other components came from Germany.

(5) The HSBC tower consists of 47 stories, which is an immense contrast to the twenty-story buildings in its vicinity. (6) The construction of other buildings nearby was impeded by the soft, water-logged ground in the area. (7) For this reason, the ground water supply had to be carefully assessed prior to construction of the HSBC building. (8) This assessment was necessary in order to ensure that subsidence, and potentially collapse of the new structure, could be averted.

5) The author of the selection uses sentence 4 in order to:

   A. reinforce the claim she makes in sentence 3.

   B. transition to the information provided in the sentence 5.

   C. provide an example for the assertion made in sentence 3.

   D. summarize the details in sentences 1 to 3.

6) Which of the following sentences would the author most likely use to continue the selection?

   A. Other buildings in the vicinity did not benefit from such an assessment.

   B. The meticulous processes involved erecting the HSBC skyscraper make its construction a truly remarkable structural feat.

C. On the other hand, subsidence was not a threat during the construction of the Chrysler and Trump buildings.

D. However, some people would argue that subsidence was not a real threat to the structure.

Read the selection and answer the questions.

The History of Polyphonic Music

(1) Polyphonic music appeared in the fifteen century during the early Renaissance period. (2) As polyphony developed, musical traditions began to change, and this meant that music began to rely on a greater range of voices.

(3) During the sixteenth century, there was an attempt to return to the tradition of Greek drama. (4) This had an extremely positive impact on the opera. (5) As a result, the opera expanded to include oratorios, which are sung musical compositions on a particular subject. (6) This phenomenon occurred in the Italian opera, and so, the opera, in turn, influenced the musical style of the early seventeenth century.

(7) The seventeenth century also witnessed the proliferation of musical instruments. (8) Musical compositions and arrangements for keyboard instruments, such as the piano and organ, thrived during this period.

(9) The eighteenth century was marked by the development of baroque music. (10) This century was dominated by two German-born geniuses: Bach and Handel. (11) These two composers wrote music in almost every genre, including opera and oratorio music.

(12) Beethoven is the crucial link between the classical and romantic periods. (13) To his compositions, he added deeper texture, meaning the depth and breadth of different types of musical sound. (14) For this reason, the music of Beethoven is commonly regarded as establishing the end of the classical period.

7) Which of the following sentences correctly cites the information from Sentence 9?

   A. It has been said that the eighteenth century was marked by the development of baroque music.

   B. Music scholars assert that baroque music was predominant in the eighteenth century.

   C. *The History of Polyphonic Music* states that baroque music pertains to the eighteenth century.

   D. "The eighteenth century was marked by the development of baroque music" (*The History of Polyphonic Music*).

8) We can surmise that the opera expanded to include oratorios in the sixteenth century because of which one of the following reasons?

   A. The genre of the opera expanded in general because of the influence of the Italian opera.

   B. Oratorios are musical compositions whose subject matter tells a story; story-telling was central to the opera, just as it was to Greek drama.

   C. Musical styles were changing as the seventeenth century approached.

   D. Actors and musicians viewed Greek drama a germane mode of performance, and oratorios were a part of Greek dramatic performances.

9) Which one of the following sentences uses correct-subject verb agreement?

   A. The students in the class who were studying advanced chemistry was required to attend a special presentation.

   B. When people go out alone after dark, they needs be alert and careful.

   C. Each and every vote counts.

   D. A bit of the furnishings were scratched and damaged.

10) Read the sentence and answer the question.

My mother's car (I crashed it last month) was still very annoyed about the money not being reimbursed and called the insurance company to complain.

Which of the following is the best revision of the sentence?

    A.   My mother was still very annoyed about the money not being reimbursed for the accident I had with her car, so she called the insurance company to complain.

    B.   My mother was still annoyed about the accident that I had with her car, and she called the insurance company to complain that the money hadn't been reimbursed.

    C.   My mother whose car I crashed last month was annoyed about the money not being reimbursed and called the insurance company to complain.

    D.   The accident I had with the car was so annoying to my mother, and she called the insurance company to say so.

11) If you wanted persuade your city's public library to purchase more books for small children who are just learning how to read, which of the following topics would be most important to address?

    A.   A personal account of the fond memories you have of learning to read.

    B.   An analysis showing that children's books cost less than other reading materials.

    C.   Research demonstrating that children who are just learning how to read are eager to access new reading materials.

    D.   A detailed complaint about the library's policies and procedures for acquiring new materials.

12) Select the best revision for the sentence that follows.

The girl's grades were outstanding, and so her university application was accepted, in spite of being only sixteen years old.

   A. Although only sixteen years old, the university accepted her application because of her outstanding grades.

   B. Although only sixteen years old, her application was accepted by the university because of her outstanding grades.

   C. Although only sixteen years old, her outstanding grades resulted in her application being accepted by the university.

   D. Although only sixteen years old, she was accepted to study at the university because of her outstanding grades.

13) Which is the best way to combine the two following sentences?

Three-dimensional graphic software has been placed on the computers in science lab. The teacher wanted us learn how to render images with the most up-to-date computer program.

   A. Three-dimensional graphic software has been placed on the computers in science lab, so the teacher wanted us learn how to render images with the most up-to-date computer program.

   B. The teacher wanted us learn how to render images with the most up-to-date computer program since three-dimensional graphic software has been placed on the computers in science lab.

   C. Three-dimensional graphic software has been placed on the computers in science lab, so that the most up-to-date computer images can be rendered.

D. Three-dimensional graphic software has been placed on the computers in science lab because the teacher wanted us to learn how to render images with the most up-to-date computer program.

14) If you were writing a personal essay for a scholarship application, which of the following would best describe the tone you should use?

   A. persuasive

   B. explanatory

   C. idiosyncratic

   D. whimsical

15) Read the sentence and choose the part that needs capitalization.

   (A) My brother (B) lives near the blue ridge mountains (C) in the western part (D) of the state.

   A. Part A

   B. Part B

   C. Part C

   D. Part D

16) Which of the following sentences is written correctly?

   A. When a person is confused about his or her identity, this is known as an identity crisis.

   B. When you are confused about your identity, this is known as an identity crisis.

   C. The experience of confusion about one's own identity, this is known as an identity crisis.

   D. The experience of confusion about one's identity is known as an identity crisis.

17) Read the sentence and answer the question.

The company was obligated to pay tax to the United States, but it moved its bank account to Belize to get around having to do so.

Which one of the following sentences expresses the same idea more concisely?

A. The company moved its bank account to Belize, so it didn't have to pay tax.

B. The company moved its bank account to Belize to evade payment of tax to the United States.

C. Because its bank account was in Belize, the company didn't have to pay US tax.

D. The company should have paid income tax, but it did not do so, because it moved its bank account to Belize in order to avoid it.

18) Chose the word or words that best complete the sentence.

_____ high time that you went to bed!

A. Its

B. It's

C. Its'

D. That was

19) After the law on compulsory use of seatbelts was revoked, it appeared that the number of automobile fatalities did not increase.

Seatbelts laws are therefore pointless.

Which of the following is the best counterargument to the selection above?

A. Most people abided by the seatbelt law when it was in effect.

B. People started to observe other traffic laws more attentively after the law on seatbelts was revoked.

- C. Nobody likes being told what to do, and the seatbelt law was no exception.
- D. There was no change in the number of people using seatbelts after the law was revoked.

20) Which one of the following sentences uses the underlined word correctly?

- A. I was depending on her help, but she baled out at the last minute.
- B. He pored over the book as he studied for the exam.
- C. She is adverse to receiving help with the project.
- D. He could not bear to listen to the loud music.

21) Choose the best order for the following sentences.

1) However, Spain seriously underestimated the military power of the United States.

2) The Spanish-American War was a relatively brief episode in United States history.

3) The conflict started when Spain declared war on the United States in April, 1898.

4) When the war ended in December of that year, Spain lost colonial rule of the Americas and a number of other territories.

- A. 2, 1, 3, 4
- B. 2, 3, 4, 1
- C. 2, 3, 1, 4
- D. 3, 4, 1, 2

22) Which of the following sentences uses clear pronouns?

- A. Her intelligence and personality make her a great candidate for the job, which is so inspiring.
- B. Many students in my class like to go to parties, although I do not like them.

C. Every person in my class has to give a presentation, so I did mine on the Civil Rights Movement.

D. My bus did not arrive at the right time for me to attend the interview, so I missed it.

23) Which of the following sentences is written correctly?

A. All of the elected officials need to be mindful of the opinions of his or her constituents.

B. Either Juan or Brett are going to the movie with me.

C. Each of the students has to hand in his or her application by the deadline.

D. A group of dissents who disagree with the government's policies have decided to revolt.

Read the selection and answer the question.

The Mechanics of Motion

The question of the mechanics of motion is complex and one that has a protracted history. Much has been discovered about gravity, defined as the force that draws objects to the earth, both before and since the British mathematician Sir Isaac Newton mused upon the subject in the 17th century. As early as the third century BC, a Greek philosopher and natural scientist named Aristotle conducted a great deal of scientific investigation into the subject. Most of Aristotle's life was devoted to the study of the objects of natural science, and it is for this work that he is most renowned. The Greek scientist wrote a tome entitled *Metaphysics*, which contains the observations that he made as a result of performing this original research in the natural sciences.

Several centuries later, in the first century AD, Ptolemy, another Greek scientist, was credited with a nascent, yet unformulated theory, that there was a force that moved toward the center of the earth, thereby holding objects on its surface. Although later ridiculed for his belief that the earth was the center of the planetary system, Aristotle's compatriot nevertheless did contribute to the development of the theory of gravity.

It was during the period called the renaissance that gravitational forces were perhaps studied most widely. An astronomer, Galileo Galilei corrected one of Aristotle's erring theories by pointing out that objects of differing weights fall to earth at the same speed. Years later, Descartes, who was known at that time as a dilettante philosopher, but was later dubbed the father of modern mathematics, held that a body in circular motion constantly strives to recede from the center. This theory added weight to the notion that bodies in motion had their own forces.

Newton took these studies a step further and used them to show that the earth's rotation does not fling bodies into the air because the force of gravity, measured by the rate of falling bodies, is greater than the centrifugal force arising from the rotation. In his first mathematical formulation of gravity, published in 1687, Newton posited that the same force that kept the moon from being propelled away from the earth also applied to gravity at the earth's surface. While this finding, termed the Law of Universal Gravitation, is said to have been occasioned by Newton's observation of the fall of an apple from a tree in the orchard at his home, in reality, the idea did not come to the scientist in a flash of inspiration, but was developed slowly over time.

Newton had the prescience to appreciate that his study was of great import for the scientific community and for society as a whole. It is because of Newton's work that we currently understand the effect of gravity on the earth as a global system. For instance, as a result of Newton's investigation into the subject of gravity, we know that geological features such as mountains and canyons can cause variances in the Earth's gravitational force. Newton is also to be acknowledged for the realization that the force of gravity becomes less robust as the distance from the equator diminishes, due to the rotation of the earth, as well as the declining mass and density of the planet from the equator to the poles.

24) Which of the following details from the selection could support an argument against the view that Ptolemy's work contributed to the development of the theory of gravity?

    A.   Ptolemy's work had some serious errors and shortcomings.

    B.   Ptolemy believed that there was a force that held objects to the earth.

C. Aristotle and Galileo also made valuable contributions to the theory of gravity.

D. Newton's work was the most important for the scientific community.

25) Choose the answer that shows the correct capitalization.

A. She loves the museum of modern art, which is located near Rockefeller center.

B. She loves the museum of modern art, which is located near Rockefeller Center.

C. She loves the museum of Modern Art, which is located near Rockefeller Center.

D. She loves the Museum of Modern Art, which is located near Rockefeller Center.

26) Choose the sentences that <u>best</u> support the following topic sentence:

A significant problem with emails and texts is that they do not always accurately express the tone that the writer has intended.

A. We have heard stories of personal break ups that have been conducted by text. In addition, employers have fired their staff by email message.

B. The tone of the message may seem clear to the person who sent it. However, sarcasm can only really be communicated in speech by the tone and inflection of the voice.

C. The recipient of an email or text message may consider this mode of communication to be insensitive or uncaring. Email would be remarkably inappropriate for events like announcing a death.

D. My sister often sends these types of messages. It really gets on my nerves.

27) Choose the words that <u>best</u> complete the sentence.

Unless he receives approval from his superiors, _____ promotion.

A. there is not going to be a

B. he will get the

C. he will not get the

D. there will be no

28) Choose the sentence that is written correctly.

A. Wanting that new car for so long, when she finally got it, she was so excited.

B. She wanted that new car for so long, and when she finally got it, she was so excited.

C. That new car, which was wanted for so long, when she finally got it, she was so excited.

D. She wanted that new car for so long, which she finally got, she was so excited.

Read the selection and answer the question.

Stone Age Artists

(1) In Southern Spain and France, Stone Age artists painted stunning drawings on the walls of caves nearly 30,000 years ago. (2) Painting pictures of the animals upon which they relied for food, the artists worked by the faint light of lamps that were made of animal fat and twigs.

(3) In addition to having to work in relative darkness, the artists had to endure great physical discomfort since the inner chambers of the caves were sometimes less than one meter in height. (4) Thus, the artists had to crouch or squat uncomfortably as they practiced their craft.

(5) Their paints were mixed from natural elements such as yellow ochre, clay, calcium carbonate, and iron oxide. (6) However, many other natural elements and minerals were not used. (7) An analysis of the cave paintings reveals that the colors of the paints used by the artists ranged from light yellow to dark black.

(8) The artists utilized ochre and manganese as engraving tools in order first to etch their outlines on the walls of the caves. (9) Before removing their lamps and leaving their creations to dry, they painted the walls with brushes of animal hair or feathers. (10) Archeologists have also discovered that ladders and scaffolding were used in higher areas of the caves.

29) You have come across the article above when doing research on Stone Age art.

Which of the following notes should be taken to reference the components of the paint?

    A.   light yellow to dark black

    B.   many other natural elements and minerals were not used

    C.   yellow ochre, clay, calcium carbonate, and iron oxide

    D.   animal fat and twigs

30) Choose the word that best completes the sentence.

Susan said that Tim and _____ saw the accident.

    A.   she

    B.   her

    C.   he

    D.   him

PERT WRITING PRACTICE TEST 2 – ANSWERS AND EXPLANATIONS

1) The correct answer is C. This is another question on pronoun-antecedent agreement. In this sentence, the word "cookies" is plural, so the plural pronoun "they" is needed. Do not let the prepositional phrase "from the shelf" confuse you. The child wants to grab the cookies, not the shelf.

2) The correct answer is C. "Covered in chocolate frosting" is a past participle phrase that describes the cake. In other words, the hostess is not covered in chocolate frosting, nor are the guests. Therefore, the words "the cake" must follow the past participle phrase. Remember that past participle phrases are those that begin with verbs that end in -ed (in the case of regular verbs). You need to be sure that you have the participle phrase next to the noun that the phrase is describing.

3) The correct answer is A. This is another question about parallel structure. Be sure that all of the items you give in a list are of the same part of speech, nouns or verbs, for example. In other words, you should not use both nouns and verbs in a list. In addition, all of the verbs you use must be in the same tense. In answer A, both verbs are in the "to" form. The other answers combine -ing and -ed verbs.

4) The correct answer is C. The selection is describing microscopes, so the statement about cameras is irrelevant and does not belong in the selection.

5) The correct answer is A. In sentence 4, the author describes the various countries involved in the project in order to reinforce the claim in sentence 3 that the project was international in nature.

6) The correct answer is B. The last sentence of a selection can be used to sum up its main points. The selection describes how the HSBC structure was erected and the problems that were faced during the construction project, so the author would likely sum up by stating that the construction of the HSBC building was a truly remarkable structural feat.

7) The correct answer is D. As we saw in test 1, for questions about appropriate citation techniques, the title of the selection needs to be stated at the beginning of the sentence or in parentheses at the end of the sentence. For this reason, answers A and B are incorrect. Sentence C is a bit too vague because it does not mention that baroque music developed during this time. Sentence D is correct because it has taken an exact quotation from the

selection, which is properly enclosed in quotation marks. Sentence D also provides the correct citation as a parenthetical item at the end of the sentence.

8) The correct answer is B. For these types of questions, you need to find the answer that is factually correct and which is as specific as possible. In order to determine whether Sentence B is correct, you need to use some deductive reasoning. Ask yourself: How are drama and the opera similar? The answer is that both art forms are used for story-telling. Alternatively, you can solve the question by process of elimination. Sentence C is far too general. Sentences A and D misstate key facts from the selection.

9) The correct answer is C. This is another question on subject-verb agreement. As we saw in practice test 1, you need to be sure to use a singular verb with a singular subject and a plural verb with a plural subject. Sentence A is incorrect because "students" is plural, while "was" is singular. Sentence B is incorrect because "they" is plural, while "needs" is singular. Finally, sentence D is incorrect because "a bit" is singular, while "were" is plural.

10) The correct answer is A. You will see at least one question on the exam like this one, which provides you with a grammatically incorrect sentence and then asks you to find the grammatically correct revision. In our selection, we need to change the subject of the sentence to "my mother" from the possessive form "My mother's car." In addition, it is best to avoid including parenthetical information in sentences, like "I crashed it last month" in our selection. Sentences B and D are not correct because they state that the accident itself annoyed the mother, when her annoyance was actually caused by the money not being reimbursed. Sentence C is incorrect because the phrase "whose car I crashed last month" needs to be offset by commas.

11) The correct answer is C. Remember that if you are trying to persuade an organization about something, it is better to bring up the positive effects of your proposal rather than mentioning negative aspects of the organization or complaining. For this reason, we can rule out answer D. Also remember that research will generally be the more authoritative than personal accounts or analyses.

12) The correct answer is D. This is similar to question 2 above. The phrase "although only sixteen years old" describes the girl, not her grades, her application, or the university.

13) The correct answer is D. This is another cause and effect question like we have seen in test 1. Remember that for questions asking you to combine two sentences, look to see whether there is a cause and effect relationship between the two sentences. In this selection, the teacher got the software because she wanted students to use the most up-to-date program. Sentences A and B state the opposite: that the teacher used the software because it was already available. Sentence C is in the passive voice and leaves out any mention of the teacher, so it is not the best answer.

14) The correct answer is A. This is another question on tone. Remember that for questions about tone, you need to think carefully about the situation. If you were writing a personal essay for a scholarship application, you would need to persuade the committee that you were worthy of the scholarship. If you only explained your background, without trying to persuade the committee, your application would not be as successful, so answer B is not the best answer. Answers C and D are not the best either. Although your application will be unique and personal, it should not be idiosyncratic or whimsical in tone.

15) The correct answer is B. This is another question about capitalizing proper nouns. Remember that proper nouns are the names of people, places, or organizations. In our selection, the Blue Ridge Mountains are a place, so part B of the selection needs to be capitalized.

16) The correct answer is D. The other answer choices are not grammatically correct because they unnecessarily use the pronoun "this" directly after the grammatical subject of the sentence.

17) The correct answer is B. Remember that when you have to restate a sentence concisely, you are looking for a word that can be used to replace a phrase in the selection. In our selection, the phrase "to get around having to do so" means that the company wanted to get around paying income tax. The word "evade" from sentence B is the most concise paraphrase of this idea.

18) The correct answer is B. You may see questions on the exam in which you have to distinguish between the use of "its" and "it's". Remember that "its" is a singular possessive pronoun, while "it's" is the contracted form of "it is." We need to place the contracted form in this sentence to come up with the colloquial phrase "it's high time."

19) The correct answer is D. When you are asked for a counterargument, you need to ask yourself what situation or evidence would cast doubt on the assertion made in the selection. If the number of fatalities did not increase after the seatbelt law was revoked, it could be because people continued to use their seatbelts on a voluntary basis.

20) The correct answer is D. This is another question on commonly-confused words. Sentence A confuses "bale" with "bail," while sentence B confuses "pore" with "pour." Pay special attention to sentence C since the confusion of "adverse" and "averse" occurs very frequently.

21) The correct answer is C. Here is another question on ordering sentences, like we have already seen in the first practice writing test. Remember that when you have to put sentences in the correct order, focus on the chronological sequence of events. Sentence 2 should be placed at the beginning of the selection because it introduces the topic of the Spanish-American War. Sentence 3 is next because it provides the date of the beginning of the conflict. Sentence 3 should be followed by sentence 1, which gives further details about the war. The selection should end with sentence 4 because it discusses the end of the war. So, the correct order is 2, 3, 1, 4.

22) The correct answer is C. This is another question on clear pronouns. For questions on clear pronouns, look at each sentence to see if there is any doubt about what the pronoun refers to. In sentence A, we do not know if the job is inspiring or if her attributes are inspiring. In sentence B, there is some doubt whether it is the parties or the students in the class that the speaker does not like. In sentence D, we do not know if the speaker missed the bus or the interview.

23) The correct answer is C. Here is another question on pronoun-antecedent agreement. Sentence A is not correct because "all" is plural, while "his or her" is singular. Sentence B is not correct because "either" is singular, while "are" is plural. Sentence D is also not correct because "group" is singular, while "have" is plural.

24) The correct answer is A. The best counterargument is the fact that Ptolemy's work had shortcomings because that creates doubt about whether any of his work could be trusted.

25) The correct answer is D. The Museum of Modern Art and Rockefeller Center are proper nouns, so they need to be capitalized as shown.

26) The correct answer is B. This rhetorical coherence question is asking you for support for the topic sentence. First of all, be sure that the other sentences address the same theme as in the

topic sentence. Sentences that are off the theme can be disregarded, so we can see that sentences A and C do not provide support. Also remember that precise examples will have a more formal tone that personal anecdotes, so for this reason, we can disregard sentence D.

27) The correct answer is C. Because the sentence begins with the word "unless," the second part of the sentence needs to have the negative form. The pronoun "he" should be reiterated for the sake of clarity.

28) The correct answer is B. We have two separate ideas in this sentence: the fact that she wanted the car and the fact that she finally got it. The word "and" should therefore be used to join the independent clauses, as shown in sentence B.

29) The correct answer is C. For questions on taking notes for research, be sure that the information from the answer choice is relevant to the topic in the question. Answer C is the only answer that describes the natural components of the paint.

30) The correct answer is A. "She" is needed since it is functioning as a grammatical subject in this part of the sentence. In other words, Mary is doing the action with Tim, so "she" should be used. If Mary were receiving an action, we would need to use the word "her." For example, Mary said that the present was given to Tim and her.

PERT READING PRACTICE TEST 3

Read the selections and answer the questions that follow.

Archeological Excavation and Interpretation

The discipline of archeology has been developing since wealthy Europeans began to plunder relics from distant lands in the early nineteenth century. Initially considered an upper-class hobby, archeology has experienced many challenges in recent years.

Before the field excavation begins, a viable site must first be located. While this process can involve assiduous research, sheer luck or an archaeologist's intuition also come into play. A logical locality to begin searching is one near sites in which artifacts have been found previously. Failing that, an archeologist must consider at a minimum whether the potential site would have been habitable for people in antiquity. Bearing in mind that modern conveniences and facilities like electricity and running water were not available in pre-historic times, the archaeologist quickly discerns that sites near rivers and caves could provide the water and shelter indispensable for day-to-day living in such inhospitable conditions.

Once the site has been located, the process of surveying commences. The ground surface of the site is then visually scrutinized to determine whether any artifacts are protruding through the soil. The archaeologist digs test pits, small holes that are equidistant to one another, in order to set out the boundaries of the larger final pit. Once these dimensions are determined, the pit is dug and sectioned off with rope or plastic.

The excavation, which is a meticulous and lengthy process, then begins in full. The archaeologist must gauge the texture and color of the soil carefully as the pit becomes deeper and deeper since variations in soil composition can be used to identify changes in climate and living conditions. It is imperative that the walls of the excavation are kept uniformly straight as the dig progresses so that these differences can be identified.

The soil that is removed from the pit is sifted through a sieve or similar device, consisting of a screen that is suspended across a metal or wooden frame. After the soil is placed in the sieve, the archaeologist gently oscillates the device. As the mechanism goes back and forth in this way, the soil falls to the ground below, while larger objects are caught in the mesh.

Throughout this process, all findings are entered in a written record to ensure that every artifact is cataloged. This activity can certainly be tedious, but it is one that is critical in order to account for each and every item properly. Each finding is placed in a plastic bag bearing a catalog number. Subsequent to this, a map of the excavation site is produced, on which the exact in-situ location of every artifact is indicated by level and position.

Finally, the arduous task of interpreting the findings ensues. During the last three centuries, various approaches have been utilized in this respect. Throughout the early 1800s, most fossil recovery took place on the European continent, resulting in an extremely Euro-centric method of examination and dissemination of findings. Lamentably, the misapprehension that the homo sapiens was European in origin began to take shape both in the archeological and wider communities at that time.

1) According to the selection, what do archeologists consider when choosing a potential site for excavation?

   A. whether research can be conducted on the site

   B. whether electricity is presently available

   C. whether the site existed in pre-historic times

   D. whether any data was previously collected from other nearby sites

2) What can be inferred about the Euro-centric method mentioned in the last paragraph of the selection?

   A. It was completely unavoidable.

   B. It took place only within a small geographical area.

   C. It was regrettable because it created cultural misunderstandings.

   D. It was widespread practice and therefore acceptable.

3) Which of the following statements is the best summary of this selection?

    A. Locating and excavating an archeological site involves meticulous and methodical processes.

    B. Protruding artifacts can create difficulties during the excavation.

    C. An archeologist has many things to consider when selecting a site.

    D. The European archeological discoveries of the 1800s should be disregarded.

Celebrate the Nobody

"Celebrity" is the term used to describe someone who is famous and attracts attention from the general public and the world's media. Traditionally, a celebrity would gain the title by his or her work or achievements in a particular field of expertise. Actors, musicians, politicians, and inventors have all become celebrities in the past. However, as the twenty-first century progresses, a new celebrity has arrived – the nobody.

As one peruses glossy TV magazines, it is easy to notice the amount of reality shows that now dominate our screens – Wife Swap, American Idol, America's Got Talent, and the reality pioneer Big Brother. The concept itself of Big Brother is everything that George Orwell warned us about: "normal" people are thrust into the limelight to be mocked, glorified, vilified, and humiliated in equal measures. And we lap it up.

Reality TV and Celebrity Status

After Big Brother first hit our screens, there were several BB series. However, the housemate that is eventually voted BB winner is not necessarily the most likely to gain fame and fortune from his or her appearance on this cultural phenomenon. The champion of Big Brother earnings, who came in at second place in her series, so far has earned an estimated net worth of three million dollars. While some vilify reality TV shows and the so-called celebrity associated with them, it must nonetheless be noted that participants can change their lives with the potential income levels to be derived from appearing on reality TV.

4) How would the writer of selection 1 most likely respond to the following statement from selection 2?: "Participants can change their lives with the potential income levels to be derived from appearing on reality TV."

   A. Reality TV participants can earn a great deal of money, but these so-called celebrities have no real achievements or expertise.

   B. Reality TV participants are foolish for wanting to earn money like this.

   C. The general public needs to stop watching reality TV shows in order to avoid money being earned in this way.

   D. Glossy TV magazines should stop promoting reality TV shows.

5) The writer of selection 2 would criticize the writer of selection 1 for:

   A. failing to analyze Big Brother in more depth.

   B. failing to mention any of the positive aspects of reality shows.

   C. calling the new celebrity a nobody.

   D. trying to classify people as "normal."

Excerpt from "On Women's Right to Vote"

Delivered by Susan B. Anthony, 1872

For any state to make sex a qualification that must ever result in the disfranchisement of one entire half of the people is a violation of the supreme law of the land. By it, the blessings of liberty are forever withheld from women and their female posterity. To them, this government has no just powers derived from the consent of the governed. To them, this government is not a democracy. It is not a republic. It is an odious aristocracy; a hateful oligarchy of sex; the oligarchs over the mother and sisters, the wife and daughters, of every household - which ordains all men sovereigns, all women subjects, carries dissension, discord, and rebellion into every home of the nation.

6) The speaker uses the words "odious," "oligarchy," and "sovereigns" to argue that:

   A. the entire populace is disenfranchised.

   B. the government is too powerful.

   C. the situation is unfair and change is necessary.

   D. proposed changes are bound to be ineffectual.

Earthquakes

Earthquakes occur when there is motion in the tectonic plates on the surface of the earth. The crust of the earth contains twelve such tectonic plates. Fault lines, the places where these plates meet, build up a great deal of pressure because the plates are constantly pressing on each other. The two plates will eventually shift or separate because the pressure on them is constantly increasing, and this build-up of energy needs to be released. When the plates shift or separate, we have an occurrence of an earthquake, also known as a seismic event.

The point where the earthquake is at is strongest is called the "epicenter." Waves of motion travel out from this epicenter, often causing widespread destruction to an area. With this likelihood for earthquakes to occur, it is essential that earthquake prediction systems are in place. The purpose of earthquake prediction systems is to give advanced warning to the population, thereby saving lives in the process. However, these prediction systems need to be more reliable in order to be of any practical use.

7) What happens immediately after the pressure on the tectonic plates has become too great?

   A. Fault lines are created.

   B. There is a build-up of energy.

   C. There is a seismic event.

   D. Waves of motion travel out from the epicenter.

8) The writer makes her final statement more compelling by preceding it by which of the following?

   A. a dispassionate, scientific explanation

   B. emotionally-evocative examples

   C. a historical account of events

   D. a prediction of a future catastrophe

The World's First Locomotive

(1) The world's first public railway carried passengers, even though it was primarily designed to transport coal from inland mines to ports on the North Sea. (2) Unveiled on September 27, 1825, the train had 32 open wagons and carried over 300 people.

(3) The locomotive steam engine was powered by what was termed the steam-blast technique. (4) The chimney of the locomotive redirected exhaust steam into the engine via a narrow pipe. (5) A draft of air followed after the steam, creating more power and speed for the engine.

(6) The train had rimmed wheels which ran atop rails that were specially designed to give the carriages a faster and smoother ride. (7) While the small carriages could hardly be termed commodious, the locomotive could accelerate to 15 miles per hour, a record-breaking speed at that time.

(8) The inventor of the locomotive, George Stephenson, subsequently revolutionized his steam engine by adding 24 further pipes. (9) Now containing 25 tubes instead of one, Stephenson's second "iron horse" was even faster and more powerful than his first creation.

9) In the selection, sentence 7:

   A. presents a slight distinction from the information in sentence 6.

   B. provides evidence that refutes sentence 6.

   C. uses a paraphrase to restate sentence 6.

   D. gives further information that supports sentence 6.

10) Why was the second locomotive that Stephenson invented an improvement on his first?

    A.   because it ran more smoothly

    B.   because it contained more pipes and tubes

    C.   because it could carry more passengers

    D.   because it ran with greater force and speed

Research on Socioeconomic Inequality

Socio-economic status, rather than intellectual ability, may be the key to a child's success later in life, according to a study by Carnegie. Let us consider two hypothetical elementary school students named John and Paul. Both of these children work hard, pay attention in the classroom, and are respectful to their teachers. However, Paul's father is a prosperous business tycoon, while John's has a menial job working in a factory. Solely owing to their disparate economic backgrounds, Paul is nearly 30 times more likely than John to land a high-flying job by the time he reaches his fortieth year, despite the similarities in their academic aptitudes. In fact, John has only a 12% chance of finding and maintaining a job that would earn him even a median-level income.

Research dealing with the economics of inequality among adults supports these findings. These studies also reveal that the economics of inequality is a trend that has become more and more pronounced in recent years. In the mid-twentieth century, the <u>mean</u> after-tax pay for a US corporate executive was more than 12 times that of the average factory worker. Today, this situation has reached a level which some economists refer to as "hyper-inequality." The press has reported that it is now common for the salary of the average CEO to be more than 100 times that of the average blue-collar employee.

Because of this and other economic dichotomies, a theoretical stance has sprung into existence, asserting that inequality is institutionalized. In keeping with this concept, some researchers argue that workers from higher socio-economic backgrounds are disproportionately compensated, even though the contribution they make to society is no more valuable than that of their lower-paid counterparts. To rectify the present imbalance caused by this economic stratification, researchers claim that economic rewards should be judged by and distributed according to the worthiness of the employment to society as a whole. Economic rewards under this framework refer not only to wages or salaries, but also to power, status, and prestige within one's community, as well as within larger society.

Cultural and critical theorists have joined in the debate that empirical researchers embarked upon decades ago. Focusing on the effect of cultural technologies and systems, they state that various forms of media promote the mechanisms of economic manipulation and oppression. Watching television, they claim, causes those of lower socio-economic class to view themselves as apolitical and powerless victims of the capitalistic machine, and thereby has a deleterious impact upon individual identity and human motivation.

At a more personal level, economic inequality also has pervasive effects on the lives of the less economically fortunate. These personal effects include the manner in which one's economic status influences musical tastes, the perception of time and space, the expression of emotion, and communication across social groups. This detrimental economic imbalance may at its most extreme form lead to differences in health and mortality in those from the lower economic levels of society.

11) The best definition of the word "mean," as it is used in the selection, is:

　　A.　unpleasant

　　B.　average

　　C.　basic

　　D.　cheap

12) In order to challenge the theory of hyper-inequality, the selection could include:

　　A.　more evidence from the Carnegie study.

　　B.　a quote from a CEO of a major corporation.

　　C.　reference to research revealing that news reports on the current level of CEO's salaries are not reliable.

　　D.　interviews with people from the lower socio-economic class.

13) Which of the following statements best expresses the main idea of the selection?

   A. Socio-economic status has wide-ranging effects on life and lifestyle, as well as on a number of personal preferences and behaviors.

   B. Socio-economic level primarily affects communication skills.

   C. Socio-economic unfairness results predominantly in lethargy among those most profoundly affected by it.

   D. Socio-economic inequality usually results in premature death to those who experience it.

Wireless Technology

Resulting from the amazing success of WAP (Wireless Application Protocol) in smart phones and hand-held devices, wireless technology can have an amazing impact on your day-to-day life. These technologies help to make the mobile information society happen by blurring the boundaries between home, the office, and the outside world.

The seamless integration and connectivity that wireless technology brings with it make it possible to work more efficiently. Business users can explore a wide range of interactive services which were difficult to envisage years ago because of the complexity involved in making such devices communicate with each other.

In addition, with wireless technologies, you can get on social media wherever you are, helping us stay connected with friends and family.

Social Media

Recent research shows that social media platforms may actually be making us antisocial. Survey results indicate that many people would prefer to interact on Facebook or Twitter, rather than see friends and family in person. The primary reason cited for this phenomenon was that one does not need to go to the effort to dress up and travel in order to use these social media platforms.

Another independent survey revealed that people often remain glued to their hand-held devices when they do go out with friends. It therefore seems that social media platforms may be having a detrimental effect on our social skills and interpersonal relationships.

14) The writer of selection 2 would probably respond to the last sentence in selection 1 by:

   A. asserting that one should try to balance time spent on social media platforms with time spent in person with loved ones.

   B. pointing out that social media platforms are very convenient.

   C. claiming that we are actually damaging relationships with our friends and family in many cases because of wireless technologies.

   D. arguing that people should leave their hand-held devices at home when going out with friends.

15) The writers of both selections would agree that:

   A. wireless technologies have impacted upon society in positive ways.

   B. social media platforms need to be used with caution.

   C. social media platforms have brought about changes to interpersonal relationships.

   D. Facebook and Twitter are useful interactive tools for business users.

Acid Rain

(1) Acid has been present in rain for millennia, naturally occurring from volcanoes and plankton. (2) However, scientific research shows that the acid content of rain has increased dramatically over the past two hundred years, in spite of humanity's recent attempts to control the problem.

(3) Rain consists of two elements, nitrogen and sulfur. (4) When sulfur is burned, it transforms into sulfur dioxide. (5) Subsequently, both sulfur dioxide and nitrogen oxide react with the water molecules in rain to form sulfuric acid and nitric acid, respectively.

(6) Factories and other enterprises have built high chimneys in an attempt to carry these gases away from urban areas. (7) Nevertheless, the effect of the structures has been to spread the gases more thinly and widely in the atmosphere, thereby exacerbating the problem.

(8) The acid in rain also emanates from automobile exhaust, domestic residences, and power stations. (9) The latter have been the culprit of the bulk of the acid in rainwater in recent years. (10) Since the pollutants are carried by the wind, countries are now experiencing acid rain from pollution that was generated in countries thousands of miles away.

16) How is the information in this selection organized?

    A. general to specific

    B. cause and effect

    C. theoretical developments and new innovations

    D. scientific background and current problems

17) Sentence 7 provides the reader with:

    A. a contrast between acid rain and gases in the atmosphere.

    B. an explanation of an unexpected and undesired outcome.

    C. a clarification of the reason for the construction of high chimneys.

    D. an example of how water molecules react with sulfur dioxide and nitrogen oxide.

Personality Theory

(1) A certain psychological theory supports the view that there are sixteen distinct personality types. (2) These sixteen personalities are based on the combination of four categories of two opposite functions which individuals use in their lives.

(3) The first of these four categories describes the way in which we relate to other people and receive our mental and social stimulation. (4) The term "extrovert" is used describe people who prefer to interact with the outside world, including interactions with other people. (5) In keeping with the vernacular use of this term, extroverts are therefore very outgoing people. (6) On the other hand, those who can be classified as "introvert" are internally-focused individuals.

(7) The individual's method of receiving information is included in the second category, in which the opposite functions are "sensing" and "intuitive." (8) Sensing involves perceiving information that is external to the individual, so "sensing" individuals function by trusting their five senses. (9) Conversely, the "intuitive" function means that a person relies on instinct, which is his or her inner voice, to process information.

(10) The third category takes a look at how we prefer to make decisions. (11) Those who come to decisions based on objective facts and logic use the "thinking" function, while those who make choices in life according to their own personal, subjective value systems use the opposite "feeling" function.

(12) The fourth and final category is concerned with how a person deals with or manages day-to-day life. (13) If a person is organized and more comfortable with schedules, timetables, and structure, he or she can be described as "judging." (14) The opposite function is "perceiving." (15) "Perceiving" individuals prefer casual, varied, and open arrangements that allow for flexibility.

(16) The combination of these four functions determines which one of the sixteen personality types the individual possesses. (17) For example, one personality type is the introverted-intuitive-feeling-judger. (18) This type of personality prefers to receive information internally, relying on instinct, basing decisions on an internal value system, and managing the outside world according to lists and schedules.

18) Which of the following sentences supports a common assumption?

    A.   Sentence 3

    B.   Sentence 5

    C.   Sentence 11

    D.   Sentence 13

19) Which of the following words <u>best</u> describes the tone of sentence 18?

    A.   droll

    B.   laconic

C. revelatory

D. instructive

Excerpt from *The Woman in White*

It was the last day of July. The long hot summer was drawing to a close; and we, the weary pilgrims of the London pavement, were beginning to think of the cloud-shadows on the corn-fields, and the autumn breezes on the sea-shore.

For my own poor part, the fading summer left me out of health and out of spirits. During the past year I had not managed my professional resources as carefully as usual; and my extravagance now limited me to the prospect of spending the autumn economically between my mother's cottage at Hampstead and my own chambers in town.

The evening, I remember, was still and cloudy. It was one of the two evenings in every week which I was accustomed to spend with my mother and my sister. So I turned my steps northward in the direction of Hampstead.

The quiet twilight was still trembling on the topmost ridges of the heath; and the view of London below me had sunk into a black gulf in the shadow of the cloudy night, when I stood before the gate of my mother's cottage. I had hardly rung the bell before the house door was opened violently; my worthy Italian friend, Professor Pesca, appeared in the servant's place; and darted out joyously to receive me, with a shrill foreign parody on English cheer.

I had first become acquainted with my Italian friend by meeting him at certain great houses where he taught his own language and I taught drawing. All I then knew of the history of his life was that he had once held a situation in the University of Padua; that he had left Italy for political reasons (the nature of which he uniformly declined to mention to any one); and that he had been for many years respectably established in London as a teacher of languages.

20) What does the narrator suggest in paragraph 2?

A. that he has run out of money

B. that he has lost all his clients

C. that he is suffering from depression

D. that he does not get along well with his mother

21) What adjective best describes the narrator's relationship with Professor Pesca?

    A. political

    B. respectable

    C. accidental

    D. collegial

The Rabies Vaccine

Best known for his process of pasteurization, or the eradication of germs in liquid substances, Louis Pasteur was also the father of the modern rabies vaccine. In December of 1880, a friend who was a veterinary surgeon gave Pasteur two rabid dogs for research purposes.

Victims of bites from rabid dogs normally showed no symptoms for three to twelve weeks. By then, however, the patient would be suffering from convulsions and delirium, and it would be too late to administer any remedy. Within days, the victim would be dead.

So-called treatments at that time consisted of burning the bitten area of skin with red-hot pokers or with carbolic acid. These "remedies" often resulted in fatal trauma to the patients.

Pasteur devoted himself to discovering a more humane and effective method of treatment for the disease.

His tests on rabid dogs confirmed that the rabies germs were isolated in the saliva or nervous systems of the animals. After many weeks of tests and experiments, Pasteur at last cultivated a vaccine from a weakened form of the rabies virus itself.

22) What are the symptoms of rabies infection, if it is left untreated?

    A. burning sensation of the skin

    B. seizures and anxiety

C. mental disturbances and physical tremors

D. muscular contractions and forgetfulness

The Giza Pyramids

The pyramids at Giza in Egypt are still among the world's largest structures, even today. Equivalent in height to 48 story buildings, the pyramids were constructed well before the wheel was invented. It is notable that the Egyptians had only the most primitive, handmade tools to complete the massive project.

Copper saws were used to cut softer stones, as well as the large wooden posts that levered the stone blocks into their final places. Wooden mallets were used to drive flint wedges into rocks in order to split them. An instrument called an adze, which was similar to what we know today as a wood plane, was employed to give wooden objects the correct finish.

The Egyptians also utilized drills that were fashioned from wood and twine. In order to ensure that the stones were level, wooden rods were joined by strips of twine to check that the surfaces of the stone blocks were flat. Finally, the stone blocks were put onto wooden rockers so that they could more easily be placed into their correct positions on the pyramid.

23) What is the writer's main purpose?

A. to give a step-by-step explanation of the construction of the Giza pyramids

B. to compare the construction of the Giza pyramids to that of modern day structures

C. to give an overview of some of the main implements that were used to construct the Giza pyramids

D. to highlight the importance of the achievement of the construction of the Giza pyramids

Excerpt from *Tess of the D'Ubervilles*

Clare, restless, went out into the dusk when evening drew on, she who had won him having retired to her chamber. The night was as sultry as the day. There was no coolness after dark unless on the grass. Roads, garden-paths, the house-fronts, the bartonwalls were warm as earths, and reflected the noontime temperature into the noctambulist's face.

He sat on the east gate of the yard, and knew not what to think of himself. Feeling had indeed smothered judgment that day. Since the sudden embrace, three hours before, the twain had kept apart. She seemed stilled, almost alarmed, at what had occurred, while the novelty, unpremeditation, mastery of circumstance disquieted him—palpitating, contemplative being that he was. He could hardly realize their true relations to each other as yet, and what their mutual bearing should be before third parties thenceforward.

The windows smiled, the door coaxed and beckoned, the creeper blushed confederacy. A personality within it was so far-reaching in her influence as to spread into and make the bricks, mortar, and whole overhanging sky throb with a burning sensibility. Whose was this mighty personality? A milkmaid's.

It was amazing, indeed, to find how great a matter the life of this place had become to him. And though new love was to be held partly responsible for this, it was not solely so. Many have learnt that the magnitude of lives is not as to their external displacements, but as to their subjective experiences. The impressionable peasant leads a larger, fuller, more dramatic life than the king. Looking at it thus, he found that life was to be seen of the same magnitude here as elsewhere.

Despite his heterodoxy, faults, and weaknesses, Clare was a man with a conscience. Tess was no insignificant creature to toy with and dismiss; but a woman living her precious life—a life which, to herself who endured or enjoyed it, possessed as great a dimension as the life of the mightiest to himself. Upon her sensations the whole world depended to Tess; through her existence all her fellow-creatures existed, to her. The universe itself only came into being for Tess on the particular day in the particular year in which she was born.

24) Which of the following is the best description of the theme of this selection?

    A.   The Peasant and the King

    B.   Clare and Tess: An Unexpected Union

    C.   Reasons to Avoid Personal Relationships

    D.   The Consequences of a Clandestine Relationship

25) Where does the story take place?

    A.   in a royal court

    B.   in a peasant's abode

    C.   in a dairy farm

    D.   in a manor house

Nutrition

Good nutrition is essential for good health. A healthy diet can help a person to maintain a good body weight, promote mental wellbeing, and reduce the risk of disease. So, you might ask, what does healthy nutrition consist of? Well, first of all, a healthy diet should include food from all of the major food groups. These food groups are carbohydrates, fruit, vegetables, dairy products, meat and other proteins, and fats and oils.

The first of the food groups, carbohydrate, includes food like potatoes, bread, and cereals. Although carbohydrates seem to have gotten bad press lately, in fact, they are an essential part of healthy nutrition because they provide the building blocks for supplying energy to the body.

The second and third food groups are fruit and vegetables, although some people would just include these as one group. It is worth pointing out here that good nutrition depends on eating a variety of fruit and vegetables. While the old adage "An apple a day keeps the doctor away" may appear to be sound advice, eating the same fruit or vegetables daily is not the best advice in reality. The amount of fruit and vegetables to be consumed is also important to bear in mind. Most medical practitioners now recommend a minimum consumption of five portions of fruit or vegetables per day.

Protein includes food such as meat and fish, as well as dairy products, like milk and cheese. There are also non-animal protein sources like tofu and nuts. For good nutrition, lean protein is better than fatty protein, so it's best to limit the consumption of red meat, rich cheeses, and cream. In addition to keeping an eye on fat intake, the amount of sugar a person eats should also be moderated.

Besides this, processed or convenience food should be avoided. Packaged food often contains chemicals, such as additives to enhance the color of the food or preservatives that give the food a longer life. Food additives are inimical to health for a number of reasons. First of all, they may be linked to disease in the long term. In addition, they may block the body's ability to absorb the essential vitamins and minerals from food that are required for healthy bodily function.

26) According to the selection, what is the primary reason why manufacturers of processed food use additives?

    A.   to make food more convenient

    B.   to improve the appearance of the food

    C.   to prevent the food from spoiling quickly

    D.   to remove harmful chemicals from the food

Vending Machines

Although there are many different types and sizes of coins in various countries, vending machines around the world operate on the same basic principles.

The first check is the slot: coins that are bent or too large will not go in. Once inside the machine, coins fall into a cradle which weighs them. If a coin is too light, it is rejected and returned to the customer.

Coins that pass the weight test are then passed along a runway beside a magnet. Electricity passes through the magnet, causing the coin to slow down in some cases. If the coin begins to slow down, its metallurgic composition has been deemed to be correct.

The coin's slow speed causes it to miss the next obstacle, the deflector. Instead, the coin falls into the "accept" channel and the customer receives the product.

27)   Based on the information in the selection, how is the metallurgical composition of a coin determined to be correct?

    A.   By its weight

    B.   By its increased velocity in the runway

    C.   By whether it runs alongside the magnet

    D.   By the electricity that has passed through the magnet

Lewis and Clark

(1) Meriwether Lewis and William Clark were perhaps the two of the most famous explorers of the American West. (2) In 1804, the two men began an expedition westward across the area of the United States that was then known as the Louisiana Territory, and along their way, they encountered unknown people and harsh climatic conditions.

(3) Lewis was born on August 18, 1774, in the state of Virginia. (4) Clark was also born in Virginia, although he was four years older than Lewis. (5) The two men met when Lewis joined the local militia, of which Clark was in command. (6) During their experiences in combat, Lewis and Clark formed a long-lasting friendship.

(7) Then-president Thomas Jefferson had been Lewis's neighbor. (8) When Lewis was a young captain in the army, he received a letter from Jefferson offering him a job in charge of an expedition to explore the Western country.

(9) On February 28, 1803, the United States Congress approved the financing for the expedition. (10) At this time, Lewis told President Jefferson that it would be preferable to have a partner for the rigorous journey westward. (11) With Jefferson's permission, Lewis offered the assignment to his friend Clark.

(12) In terms of their backgrounds, abilities, and interests, Lewis and Clark had a great deal in common. (13) They both possessed many traits that would prove to be crucial for such a

daunting expedition: they were both known as lovers of adventure, and because of their time in the army, they were seen to be calm under pressure and able to make important decisions quickly.

(14) The journey that Lewis and Clark made was more than 8,000 miles in length and lasted for nearly two and a half years. (15) The team charted their course by following the Missouri River, and they were responsible for discovering the Northwest Passage. (16) When their expedition had safely concluded, President Jefferson purchased the Louisiana Territory for fifteen million dollars. (17) Thus, the most important land acquisition in the history of the United States took place.

28) Which numbered sentence provides an opinion rather than a fact?

　　A.　Sentence 6

　　B.　Sentence 10

　　C.　Sentence 13

　　D.　Sentence 17

Skill Recall

Many skills can be easily recalled once they have been learned.

Riding a bike is easy, even if you haven't done it for years.

29) What does the second sentence do?

　　A.　It sums up the points raised in the first sentence.

　　B.　It presents a solution to the problem mentioned in the first sentence.

　　C.　It provides a specific example for the general claim made in the first sentence.

　　D.　It repeats the same idea as stated in the first sentence.

Excerpt from *Culture and Imperialism*

By Edward Said, 1993

"All knowledge that is about human society, and not about the natural world, is historical knowledge, and therefore rests upon judgment and interpretation. This is not to say that facts or data are non-existent, but that facts get their importance from what is made of them in interpretation, for interpretations depend very much on who the interpreter is, who he or she is addressing, what his or her purpose is, and at what historical moment the interpretation takes place."

30) The selection suggests that historical knowledge:

    A. diverges from knowledge about human society.

    B. is distinct from facts and data.

    C. hinges on the analyses and opinions of scholars and historians.

    D. derives from purposes that are dubious from a historical perspective.

PERT READING PRACTICE TEST 3 – ANSWERS AND EXPLANATIONS

1) The correct answer is D. When choosing a potential site for excavation, archeologists consider whether any data was previously collected from other nearby sites. Paragraph 2 of the selection states: "A logical locality to begin searching is one near sites in which artifacts have been found previously."

2) The correct answer is C. The Euro-centric method was regrettable because it created cultural misunderstandings. We can make this determination because of the word "lamentably" in the last paragraph.

3) The correct answer is A. The best summary of the selection is that locating and excavating an archeological site involves meticulous and methodical processes. The selection begins by talking about how a site is located, before devoting the majority of the remainder of the selection to describing the excavation process.

4) The correct answer is A. The writer of selection 1 states that "traditionally, a celebrity would gain the title by his or her work or achievements in a particular field of expertise," so he would agree with answer A.

5) The correct answer is B. The writer of selection 2 describes how participants in reality shows can "change their lives with the potential income levels to be derived from appearing on reality TV." This is an assertion about the positive, life-changing aspects of reality television. The writer of selection 1 fails to discuss any positive aspects of reality TV.

6) The correct answer is C. The speaker uses the words "odious," "oligarchy," and "sovereigns" to argue that the situation is unfair and change is necessary. We know that the speaker thinks the situation is unfair because she says that "the blessings of liberty are forever withheld" from women if they cannot vote. Therefore, she is arguing for change.

7) The correct answer is C. Focus on the last two sentences of the first paragraph. From the second to the last sentence, we read that the "plates will eventually shift or separate because the pressure on them is constantly increasing." We go on to read in the final sentence of the paragraph that the separation of the plates is "known as a seismic event."

8) The correct answer is A. The writer's final statement is that "prediction systems need to be more reliable in order to be of any practical use." The writer precedes this with a scientific explanation of how waves travel out from the epicenter of the earthquake.

9) The correct answer is D. Sentence 6 explains that the wheels gave "the carriages a faster and smoother ride." Sentence 7 gives further information about the speed of the train when it states that "the locomotive could accelerate to 15 miles per hour."

10) The correct answer is D. The last sentence of the paragraph states that "Stephenson's second 'iron horse' was even faster and more powerful than his first creation." In other words, we can conclude that the second locomotive was an improvement because it ran with greater force and speed that the first one did.

11) The correct answer is B. The selection states that "the mean after-tax pay for a US corporate executive was more than 12 times that of the average factory worker." Because the paragraph is talking about different classes of workers and their pay rates in general, we know that the word "mean" is referring to a mathematical average.

12) The correct answer is C. The question is asking you for evidence needed in order to challenge a theory, rather than to support it. The selection argues that "the press has reported that it is now common for the salary of the average CEO to be more than 100 times that of the average blue-collar employee." So, research revealing that these reports are not reliable would cast doubt on the theory of hyper-inequality.

13) The correct answer is A. The main idea of the selection is that socio-economic status has wide-ranging effects on life and lifestyle, as well as on a number of personal preferences and behaviors. The selection talks about how socio-economic status affects a person's life. The main idea is reiterated in the last paragraph when it states: "These personal effects include the manner in which one's economic status influences musical tastes, the perception of time and space, the expression of emotion, and communication across social groups."

14) The correct answer is C. The writer of selection 2 explains how people are more inclined to stay at home to chat on social media than to go out with friends and how people are glued to their hand-held devices even when they are out with friends. These are two detrimental impacts of social media on interpersonal relationships.

15) The correct answer is C. The writer of selection 1 describes the positive changes, while the writer of selection 2 describes the negative changes.

16) The correct answer D. The technical language in paragraph 2 shows that a scientific explanation is being provided. Paragraph 3 talks about "exacerbating the problem," indicating

that current problems are being discussed. Accordingly, the first part of the selection focuses on from scientific background, while the remainder of the selection discusses current problems.

17) The correct answer is B. Spreading the gases more thinly and widely in the atmosphere is an undesired and unexpected outcome. We know that it is unexpected because of the word "nevertheless" at the beginning of the sentence. We know that it is undesired because of the phrase "thereby exacerbating the problem."

18) The correct answer is B. Sentence 5 states: "In keeping with the vernacular use of this term, extroverts are therefore very outgoing people." The word "vernacular" means the way in which something is expressed in common language, so the phrase "in keeping with the vernacular use" means that it is a common assumption that extroverts are very outgoing people.

19) The correct answer is D. The sentence is instructive in tone because it is explaining the aspects of a certain personality type. We can rule out the other answer choices by process of elimination: "droll" means humorous; "laconic" means to use few words, and "revelatory" means to divulge secret information.

20) The correct answer is A. The narrator states in paragraph 2 that he needs to spend the autumn "economically," so the reader can surmise that he is having financial problems. Note that the narrator mentions that he is "out of spirits," but this condition is not as serious as suffering from depression.

21) The correct answer is D. "Collegial" means acting like colleagues, or people who work in the same profession. Paragraph 5 of the text explains that Professor Pesca and the narrator met when they were teachers, so the two characters would have been colleagues.

22) The correct answer is C. Paragraph 2 states: "Victims of bites from rabid dogs normally showed no symptoms for three to twelve weeks. By then, however, the patient would be suffering from convulsions and delirium, and it would be too late to administer any remedy." "Delirium" means mental disturbances and "convulsions" means physical tremors.

23) The correct answer is C. The writer's main purpose is to give an overview of some of the main implements that were used to construct the Giza pyramids. The main purpose of the passage is implied in the last sentence of the first paragraph: "It is notable that the Egyptians had only the most primitive, handmade tools to complete the massive project."

24) The correct answer is B. The selection describes the interaction between the characters Clare and Tess, so "Clare and Tess: An Unexpected Union" is the best description of the theme of the selection. Answer A is too specific, while answers C and D are too general.

25) The correct answer is C. We know that the story takes place in a dairy farm because Clare confesses that he has fallen in love with a milkmaid at the end of paragraph 3.

26) The correct answer is B. According to the passage, the primary reason why manufacturers of processed food use additives is to improve the appearance of the food. In the first sentence of paragraph 2, we see that additives "enhance the color of the food."

27) The correct answer is D. The metallurgical composition of a coin is determined to be correct by the electricity that has passed through the magnet. Paragraph 3 states: "Electricity passes through the magnet, causing the coin to slow down in some cases. If the coin begins to slow down, its metallurgic composition has been deemed to be correct." That is to say, the coin slows down because of the electricity that has passed through the magnet.

28) The correct answer is D. Sentence 17 states: "the most important land acquisition in the history of the United States took place." The phrase "most important" expresses an opinion.

29) The correct answer is C. The general concept of skill recall is mentioned in the first sentence, while the specific example of recalling the skill of how to ride a bicycle is stated in the second sentence.

30) The correct answer is C. The selection suggests that historical knowledge hinges on the analyses and opinions of scholars and historians when it claims that historical knowledge "rests upon judgment and interpretation."

PERT WRITING PRACTICE TEST 3

Read the selection and answer the question.

Lewis and Clark

(1) Meriwether Lewis and William Clark were perhaps the two of the most famous explorers of the American West. (2) In 1804, the two men began an expedition westward across the area of the United States that was then known as the Louisiana Territory, and along their way, they encountered unknown people and harsh climatic conditions.

(3) Lewis was born on August 18, 1774, in the state of Virginia. (4) Clark was also born in Virginia, although he was four years older than Lewis. (5) The two men met when Lewis joined the local militia, of which Clark was in command. (6) During their experiences in combat, Lewis and Clark formed a long-lasting friendship.

(7) Then-president Thomas Jefferson had been Lewis's neighbor. (8) When Lewis was a young captain in the army, he received a letter from Jefferson offering him a job in charge of an expedition to explore the Western country.

(9) On February 28, 1803, the United States Congress approved the financing for the expedition. (10) At this time, Lewis told President Jefferson that it would be preferable to have a partner for the rigorous journey westward. (11) With Jefferson's permission, Lewis offered the assignment to his friend Clark.

(12) In terms of their backgrounds, abilities, and interests, Lewis and Clark had a great deal in common. (13) They both possessed many traits that would prove to be crucial for such a daunting expedition: they were both known as lovers of adventure, and because of their time in the army, they were seen to be calm under pressure and able to make important decisions quickly.

(14) The journey that Lewis and Clark made was more than 8,000 miles in length and lasted for nearly two and a half years. (15) The team charted their course by following the Missouri River, and they were responsible for discovering the Northwest Passage. (16) When their expedition had safely concluded, President Jefferson purchased the Louisiana Territory for fifteen million

dollars. (17) Thus, the most important land acquisition in the history of the United States took place.

1) The author of the selection uses sentence 13 in order to:

   A. summarize her previous points.

   B. transition to a new paragraph.

   C. inspire a sense of adventure in her readers.

   D. exemplify the assertion stated in sentence 12.

2) Select the sentence that uses correct subject-verb agreement.

   A. A good set of golf clubs cost more than $1,000.

   B. The police officer, as well as his assistant, were shot.

   C. Joey and Mika often jog together.

   D. Your health and wellbeing is in your own hands.

3) Which of the following sentences uses the underlined word correctly?

   A. Her behavior was so bazaar yesterday.

   B. She was accused of conducting illicit financial transactions online.

   C. He gave me a nice complement about my new sweater.

   D. You will need an envelop if you are going to mail that letter.

Read the selection and answer the question.

Archeological Excavation and Interpretation

The discipline of archeology has been developing since wealthy Europeans began to plunder relics from distant lands in the early nineteenth century. Initially considered an upper-class hobby, archeology has experienced many challenges in recent years.

Before the field excavation begins, a viable site must first be located. While this process can involve assiduous research, sheer luck or an archaeologist's intuition also come into play. A logical locality to begin searching is one near sites in which artifacts have been found previously. Failing that, an archeologist must consider at a minimum whether the potential site would have been habitable for people in antiquity. Bearing in mind that modern conveniences and facilities like electricity and running water were not available in pre-historic times, the archaeologist quickly discerns that sites near rivers and caves could provide the water and shelter indispensable for day-to-day living in such inhospitable conditions.

Once the site has been located, the process of surveying commences. The ground surface of the site is then visually scrutinized to determine whether any artifacts are protruding through the soil. The archaeologist digs test pits, small holes that are equidistant to one another, in order to set out the boundaries of the larger final pit. Once these dimensions are determined, the pit is dug and sectioned off with rope or plastic.

The excavation, which is a meticulous and lengthy process, then begins in full. The archaeologist must gauge the texture and color of the soil carefully as the pit becomes deeper and deeper since variations in soil composition can be used to identify changes in climate and living conditions. It is imperative that the walls of the excavation are kept uniformly straight as the dig progresses so that these differences can be identified.

The soil that is removed from the pit is sifted through a sieve or similar device, consisting of a screen that is suspended across a metal or wooden frame. After the soil is placed in the sieve, the archaeologist gently oscillates the device. As the mechanism goes back and forth in this way, the soil falls to the ground below, while larger objects are caught in the mesh.

Throughout this process, all findings are entered in a written record to ensure that every artifact is cataloged. This activity can certainly be tedious, but it is one that is critical in order to account for each and every item properly. Each finding is placed in a plastic bag bearing a catalog number. Subsequent to this, a map of the excavation site is produced, on which the exact in-situ location of every artifact is indicated by level and position.

Finally, the arduous task of interpreting the findings ensues. During the last three centuries, various approaches have been utilized in this respect. Throughout the early 1800s, most fossil recovery took place on the European continent, resulting in an extremely Euro-centric method of examination and dissemination of findings. Lamentably, the misapprehension that the homo sapiens was European in origin began to take shape both in the archeological and wider communities at that time.

4) Which of the following sentences best paraphrases the steps involved in the excavation process?

    A. The archeologist must check the composition of the soil while the dig progresses, as well as ensuring that the sides of the pit are uniform and that the soil and artifacts removed from the pit are handled correctly.

    B. The archeologist needs to verify the texture of the soil so that the pit walls can be kept straight. He or she then needs to catalog the artifacts that have been recovered from the pit.

    C. After digging the pit, the archeologist needs to sift through the soil in order to locate the artifacts.

    D. Keeping the pit walls uniform, the archeologist searches through the soil with a sieve and oscillates the devise.

Read the selection and answer the question.

Acid Rain

(1) Acid has been present in rain for millennia, naturally occurring from volcanoes and plankton. (2) However, scientific research shows that the acid content of rain has increased dramatically over the past two hundred years, in spite of humanity's recent attempts to control the problem.

(3) Rain consists of two elements, nitrogen and sulfur. (4) When sulfur is burned, it transforms into sulfur dioxide. (5) Subsequently, both sulfur dioxide and nitrogen oxide react with the water molecules in rain to form sulfuric acid and nitric acid, respectively.

(6) Factories and other enterprises have built high chimneys in an attempt to carry these gases away from urban areas. (7) Nevertheless, the effect of the structures has been to spread the gases more thinly and widely in the atmosphere, thereby exacerbating the problem.

(8) The acid in rain also emanates from automobile exhaust, domestic residences, and power stations. (9) The latter have been the culprit of the bulk of the acid in rainwater in recent years. (10) Since the pollutants are carried by the wind, countries are now experiencing acid rain from pollution that was generated in countries thousands of miles away.

5) Which of the following sentences demonstrates the appropriate way to cite the information in sentence 5?

   A. It is well known that sulfuric acid and nitric acid are formed from the water molecules in rain.

   B. Scientific experiments tell us that both sulfur dioxide and nitrogen oxide react with the water molecules in rain to form sulfuric acid and nitric acid, respectively.

   C. Sulfur dioxide reacts with rain to create sulfuric acid, while nitric acid is formed when nitrogen oxide is combined with rain water (*Acid Rain*).

   D. According to the information in the *Acid Rain* publication, sulfuric acid and nitric acid are formed when sulfur dioxide and nitrogen oxide react with the water molecules in rain.

6) Read the sentence and choose the part that needs capitalization.

   (A) The administrative assistant (B) of the company (C) used to be an agent (D) with the federal bureau of investigation.

   A. Part A
   B. Part B
   C. Part C
   D. Part D

7) Which of the following sentences uses correct parallel structure?

   A. I woke up, got out of bed, and drank a coffee.
   B. I went to the concert with Marti, Akiko, and Sarah was also there.

C. I ordered my meal, waited for my drink, and it took so long for it to come.

D. The teacher explained the situation to me, clearly, calmly, and without becoming impatient.

Read the selection and answer the questions.

Organic Farming

(1) Organic farming and organic produce create many positive outcomes for the environment. (2) Most mainstream American consumers have reservations about organic food.

(3) The first drawback that consumers perceive is of course the cost. (4) Consumers with higher income levels can afford organically-grown food, but many people simply do not believe that the potential benefits are worth the added expense.

(5) There are also concerns about the safety of organic food due to using cow manure and other animal waste as fertilizer. (6) Take the case of windfall apples, which are apples that fall off the tree. (7) These apples can be contaminated by the cow manure, and this contamination occurs because the manure contains a virulent bacterium. (8) This bacterium is known as e-coli.

(9) Finally, some people are reluctant to purchase organic food because they believe that it spoils too quickly. (10) Therefore, it may be quite some time before the purchase of organic food becomes the norm in American households.

8) What is the best way to revise and combine sentences 1 and 2?

A. Organic farming and organic produce create many positive outcomes for the environment, most mainstream American consumers have reservations about organic food.

B. Most mainstream American consumers have reservations about organic food, organic farming and organic produce create many positive outcomes for the environment.

C. While organic farming and organic produce create many positive outcomes for the environment, most mainstream American consumers have reservations about organic food.

D. Organic farming and organic produce create many positive outcomes for the environment, even though most mainstream American consumers have reservations about organic food.

9) Which of the following details from the selection least supports the conclusion that "it may be quite some time before the purchase of organic food becomes the norm in American households"?

A. Organic farming and organic produce create many positive outcomes for the environment.

B. The first drawback that consumers perceive is of course the cost.

C. There are also concerns about the safety of organic food due to using cow manure and other animal waste as fertilizer.

D. Some people are reluctant to purchase organic food because they believe that it spoils too quickly.

10) You are texting a close friend of yours to ask for advice on your homework assignment. Which of the following words would best describe the tone of your message?

A. academic

B. informal

C. supportive

D. altruistic

11) Choose the sentence that is written correctly.

   A.   Not wanting to buy an e-book, a paperback book was my preferred choice.

   B.   Being the best-seller of the month, I decided to buy the paperback.

   C.   The paperback's purchase was a logical choice on my behalf.

   D.   While at the mall today, I purchased a paperback book.

12) Choose the best order for the following sentences.

   1)   Saskatchewan, a province in central Canada, is bordered by Alberta and Manitoba.

   2)   This means that the province is one of the most ethnically diverse in the nation.

   3)   Saskatchewan was settled in 1774, although it had been inhabited for many years before then.

   4)   Research demonstrates that various indigenous peoples have inhabited the province, including the Blackfeet, Cree, and Atsina tribes.

   A.   1, 4, 3, 2

   B.   1, 3, 2, 4

   C.   1, 3, 4, 2

   D.   3, 1, 4, 2

13) Read the sentence and answer the question.

   She did not directly say what she meant. She expected me to judge how she felt from her tone of voice.

   Which of the following revisions expresses the same idea more concisely?

   A.   She was just beating around the bush.

   B.   She spoke to me harshly, without coming to the point.

C. I was supposed to judge her attitude indirectly.

D. She expected me to infer what she meant.

14) Choose the words that best complete the sentence.

_____ at the airport when Paula's flight landed.

A. We just arrived

B. We had just arrived

C. Just as we had arrived

D. Just as we were arriving

15) Which of the following sentences is written correctly?

A. We were going to go away on vacation. And then our plans changed.

B. We were going to go away on vacation, then our plans changed.

C. We were going to go away on vacation and then our plans changed.

D. We were going to go away on vacation, and then our plans changed.

16) Which of the following sentences uses correct parallel structure?

A. Ahmed's favorite hobbies are to read and to swim.

B. Ahmed's favorite hobbies are to read and swimming.

C. Ahmed's favorite hobbies are reading and swimming.

D. Ahmed's favorite hobbies are reading and to swim.

17) Which of the following is the best counterargument to the selection?

After increasing the amount of math homework her students had to do, Mrs. Smith noticed that their grades on the college entrance exam were much higher than those of the students the previous year.

A. Most students do not like doing math homework, so they could not have studied with much enthusiasm.

B. Research shows that the college entrance exams were slightly less difficult this year than last year.

C. Mrs. Smith was responsible for assigning the homework, so her viewpoint is not unbiased.

D. The students also did a great deal of studying for the college entrance exam that Mrs. Smith had not assigned.

18) Which of the following sentences is written correctly?

A. Exasperated, Bill finally lost his temper with his unruly children.

B. Bill was exasperated, finally lost his temper with his unruly children.

C. Bill, exasperated, and finally lost his temper with his unruly children.

D. Exasperating by their behavior, Bill finally lost his temper with his unruly children.

19) Choose the words that best complete the sentence.

He was planning on finding a new _____ would accommodate all of his oversized furniture.

A. apartment, that

B. apartment. One that

C. apartment that

D. apartment so that

20) Which of the following sentences uses clear pronouns?

A. Sam told me that William said that the store was closed, but I did not believe him.

B. My wallet was inside my backpack when it was stolen.

C. Tourists love to go to Vale, Colorado, in the wintertime, which is so wonderful.

D. When my friends call me, they usually make me laugh.

21) Which of the following sentences is written correctly?

   A. If my brothers need help, he can just drop by anytime.

   B. The band members worked together to ensure that they had a good performance.

   C. The town council was pleased when it got the approval for their new offices to be built.

   D. A person should eat well and get enough sleep in order to improve their health.

22) You are writing a paper about the increase in noise pollution in your city. Which of the following items would provide the most authoritative evidence for your assignment?

   A. Reference to a research report published by the city council indicating that noise pollution has increased in the city.

   B. A quotation from a research study by an independent firm indicating that noise pollution in the city increased fifty percent over last year.

   C. Interviews with local business people who have suffered adverse effects from the increase in noise in the city.

   D. A list of the potential health risks posed by the increase in noise in the city.

23) Read the sentence and then answer the question.

   The client's claim the lawyer defended last month was very happy with the outcome of the case and she wrote a positive online review about the law firm.

   A. The client (whose claim the lawyer defended last month) was so happy with the outcome of the case that she wrote a positive online review about the law firm.

   B. The client's claim the lawyer defended last month was very happy with the outcome of the case, and so she wrote a positive online review about the law firm to say so.

C. The client's claim was very happy with the outcome of the case by the lawyer who defended it who last month and she wrote a positive online review about the law firm.

D. The client was very happy with the outcome of her case, which the lawyer defended last month, so she wrote a positive online review about the law firm.

24) Which of the following sentences is punctuated correctly?

A. "I can't believe you won the lottery", Sarah exclaimed.

B. "I can't believe you won the lottery." Sarah exclaimed.

C. "I can't believe you won the lottery!" Sarah exclaimed.

D. "I can't believe you won the lottery" Sarah exclaimed.

25) Choose the words that best complete the sentence.

In spite of _____ failed the exam.

A. he studied hard, he

B. studied hard, he

C. he studying hard, he

D. studying hard, he

26) Which of the following sentences is incorrect?

A. If stealing money from your employer, you could be charged with the crime of embezzlement.

B. If caught stealing money from your employer, you could be charged with the crime of embezzlement.

C. If you steal money from your employer, you could be charged with the crime of embezzlement.

D. Stealing money from one's employer is the crime of embezzlement.

27) If you wanted to give a speech to persuade the school board to increase the variety of food served for school lunches, which of the following would be the best topic to address?

    A. Some students eat packed lunches in order to avoid eating the food the school serves.

    B. There will be a noticeable cost to the school associated with serving an increased variety of food.

    C. Some students will never be satisfied with the school meals, regardless of what is served.

    D. There are many health benefits associated with eating a larger variety of food.

Read the selection and answer the question.

Nutrition

Good nutrition is essential for good health. A healthy diet can help a person to maintain a good body weight, promote mental wellbeing, and reduce the risk of disease. So, you might ask, what does healthy nutrition consist of? Well, first of all, a healthy diet should include food from all of the major food groups. These food groups are carbohydrates, fruit, vegetables, dairy products, meat and other proteins, and fats and oils.

The first of the food groups, carbohydrate, includes food like potatoes, bread, and cereals. Although carbohydrates seem to have gotten bad press lately, in fact, they are an essential part of healthy nutrition because they provide the building blocks for supplying energy to the body.

The second and third food groups are fruit and vegetables, although some people would just include these as one group. It is worth pointing out here that good nutrition depends on eating a variety of fruit and vegetables. While the old adage "An apple a day keeps the doctor away" may appear to be sound advice, eating the same fruit or vegetables daily is not the best advice in reality. The amount of fruit and vegetables to be consumed is also important to bear in mind.

Most medical practitioners now recommend a minimum consumption of five portions of fruit or vegetables per day.

Protein includes food such as meat and fish, as well as dairy products, like milk and cheese. There are also non-animal protein sources like tofu and nuts. For good nutrition, lean protein is better than fatty protein, so it's best to limit the consumption of red meat, rich cheeses, and cream. In addition to keeping an eye on fat intake, the amount of sugar a person eats should also be moderated.

Besides this, processed or convenience food should be avoided. Packaged food often contains chemicals, such as additives to enhance the color of the food or preservatives that give the food a longer life. Food additives are inimical to health for a number of reasons. First of all, they may be linked to disease in the long term. In addition, they may block the body's ability to absorb the essential vitamins and minerals from food that are required for healthy bodily function.

28) Which of the following sentences would the author most likely use to continue the selection?

    A. Vitamins and minerals are absorbed into the body when food enters the stomach, where food molecules are broken down by stomach acid, before passing into the intestine.

    B. Accordingly, the avoidance of fat, sugar, and food additives, as well as the consumption of a well-balanced diet will help the body to function at an optimal level.

    C. Disease can also be avoided through frequent hand washing and good hygiene.

    D. Therefore, you may need to take a vitamin supplement.

29) Read the sentence and choose the part that needs capitalization.

(A) The law (B) on capital punishment (C) is a matter for the state government, (D) rather than the supreme court.

    A. Part A

B. Part B

C. Part C

D. Part D

30) Choose the words that best complete the sentence.

Jane is the _____ her four sisters.

A. taller of

B. taller than

C. most tall of

D. tallest of

PERT WRITING PRACTICE TEST 3 – ANSWERS AND EXPLANATIONS

1) The correct answer is D. In sentence 12, the writer states that Lewis and Clark had a great deal in common. In sentence 13, she gives examples of some of the traits they had in common. Note that the word "exemplify" means to give examples.

2) The correct answer is C. This is a question on subject-verb agreement. "Joey and Mika" is plural, so the plural verb "jog" is used correctly in sentence C.

3) The correct answer is B. "Illicit" means illegal. Do not confuse "illicit" with the verb "elicit." Sentence A confuses "bazaar" and "bizarre." Sentence C confuses "complement" and "compliment," while sentence D confuses "envelop" and "envelope."

4) The correct answer is A. For paraphrasing questions, you need to ensure that the restatement is as correctly stated and as close to the original as possible. Sentence B is incorrect because it implies that the texture of the soil impacts upon the uniformity of the walls. Sentences C and D are not the best because they both fail to mention the detail of checking the composition of the soil.

5) The correct answer is C. Sentences A and B fail to provide the title of the selection in the citation, while parts of sentence D have been copied exactly from the text, without enclosing the words in quotation marks.

6) The correct answer is D. The Federal Bureau of Investigation is also known as the FBI. It is the name of an organization, so it is a proper noun and needs to be capitalized.

7) The correct answer is A. Sentence A is correct because it uses verbs, all of which are in the simple past tense (woke up, got out, and drank).

8) The correct answer is C. The selection is emphasizing the reservations that people have about organic food, so the clause of the sentence about the positive outcomes of organic food needs to be subordinated as shown in sentence C. Sentence D incorrectly subordinates the clause about the reservations that people have about organic produce. Sentences A and B are not grammatically correct.

9) The correct answer is A. Sentence A mentions the positive aspects of our topic, but the selection focuses on the negative aspects. Therefore, sentence A provides the least support for the selection.

10) The correct answer is B. If you are texting a friend, your tone would be informal. You are the one asking for help, so while your friend's response to you might be supportive or altruistic, your text would not have either of those tones.

11) The correct answer is D. The phrase "while at the mall" modifies the pronoun "I," so sentence D is correct as written. The other sentences have misplaced modifiers.

12) The correct answer is C. Sentence 1 introduces the topic of Saskatchewan. Sentence 3 gives the founding date of the province. Sentence 4 should be next because it continues the idea of inhabitation from the previous sentence. Sentence 2 is the conclusion, so it is last.

13) The correct answer is D. The word "infer" means to judge someone's attitude from their tone of voice or from what they state indirectly.

14) The correct answer is B. This sentence contains the word "just" to indicate a recently completed action. When a compound sentence contains the word "just" to describe an action that has recently been completed, the past perfect tense [had + past participle] should be used in the part of the sentence containing the word "just."

15) The correct answer is D. This question is about the use of punctuation. "Then our plans changed" is an independent clause. It has a grammatical subject [our plans] and a verb [changed]. "And" is a coordinating conjunction that is needed in order to combine phrases or clauses within a sentence. Since "and" is a conjunction, we should avoid beginning sentences with "and." So, the word "and" should be included within a single sentence and preceded by a comma.

16) The correct answer is C. This question is about gerunds, also known as -ing words or verbal nouns. Note that the -ing form is usually used when discussing activities or hobbies. So, the -ing form needs to be used in both parts of the sentence in order to achieve the correct parallel structure.

17) The correct answer is B. The assertion that exams were easier would cast doubt on the notion that the students were better prepared for the test. In other words, their scores would have been higher anyway if the exam was not as difficult as previous exams.

18) The correct answer is A. "Exasperated" is a past participle phrase that describes Bill. So, the sentence is correct as it is written in answer A.

19) The correct answer is C. The words "that would accommodate all of his oversized furniture" form a dependent relative clause. A dependent relative clause containing "that" is not preceded by a comma.

20) The correct answer is D. Sentence D is correct because the pronoun "they" clearly refers to "friends." In sentence A, it is not clear whether the speaker did not believe William or Sam. In sentence B, we cannot be sure whether the wallet or the backpack was stolen. In sentence C, we do not know if the wintertime is wonderful or if Vale is wonderful.

21) The correct answer is B. "Members" is plural, so the plural pronoun "they" is used correctly in the second part of the sentence.

22) The correct answer is B. For questions like this one, remember that reference to research will be the most authoritative and persuasive evidence. Reference that is conducted independently will have much more authority than research that has been conducted by the organization on its own behalf, so answer B is better than answer A.

23) The correct answer is D. This selection incorrectly uses "the client's claim" as the subject of the sentence, rather than "the client." Sentences B and C have also incorrectly used "the client's claim" as the grammatical subject. Sentence A is not the best answer because it is preferable to avoid the practice of placing information in parentheses within sentences.

24) The correct answer is C. Punctuation should be enclosed within the final quotation mark when giving dialogue. The word "exclaimed" shows that the exclamation point is needed.

25) The correct answer is D. The phrase "in spite of" must be followed by a noun or noun phrase. "In spite of" should not be followed by a clause. The -ing form "studying" is used as a gerund (a verbal noun) in this sentence, so D is the correct answer.

26) The correct answer is A. In other words, sentence A is written incorrectly. This question tests your knowledge of conditional sentence structures. Conditional sentences often begin with the word "if." Conditional sentences may address hypothetical or imaginary situations. This sentence describes the crime of embezzlement, which is a hypothetical situation. For conditional sentence like these, the simple present tense needs to be used in the "if" clause, like "caught" in sentence B and "steal" in sentence C. Sentence A incorrectly uses the -ing form in the if clause, so answer A is incorrect. Sentence D is correct as written because it does not begin with the word "if."

27) The correct answer is D. The health benefits are one positive aspect of serving an increased variety of food. The other sentences bring up negative points, which would not be as persuasive in this case.

28) The correct answer is B. Remember that the last sentence of a selection can be used to sum up the main points. Sentence B concludes the selection by reiterating the points about fat, sugar, and food additives. The other sentences bring up new points, which should not normally be raised when concluding a selection.

29) The correct answer is D. The Supreme Court is a proper noun, so it has to be capitalized.

30) The correct answer is D. This question tests your knowledge of the comparative and superlative forms. Use the comparative form (-er) when comparing two things. If you are comparing more than two things, you must use the superlative form (-est).

Made in the
USA
Columbia, SC